Panzer IV, 1939–1945, the account of the Panzerkampfwagen IV (PzKpfw IV), is an illustrated record of one of the foremost fighting machines in the German arsenal. Its ordnance inventory designation was SdKfz 161 and during the war over 8,000 were built. For the majority of the war this tank was certainly a match for its opponents' heavy tanks and quickly and effectively demonstrated its superiority on the battlefield. In fact it played a crucial part in the desperate attempt to halt the Soviet juggernaut, and was also used with deadly effect in the West performing both defensive and offensive operations.

From the victorious days in Poland in 1939 until the last-ditch defensive battles fought out during the last days of the Third Reich in 1945, the book reveals the numerous variants that saw action. Using a host of rare and previously unpublished photographs, many of which have come from the albums of individuals who took part in the war, it presents a unique visual account of the most popular German tank of the Second World War.

With informative captions and text the book analyzes the development of the vehicle markings and shows how the PzKpfw IV was camouflaged. It details many of the German tank colour variations from the early war, to the North African campaign, and to the final desperate months of the war. Throughout this period from 1939 to 1945 it describes the summer and winter camouflage schemes, camouflage netting and tarpaulins, foliage – the *zimmerit* – and shows various tactical signs and insignia of specific Panzer forces. With photographs and illustrations each section of the book details the various Panzer variants that went into production and saw action on the battlefield. From the PzKpfw IV Ausf A to the Ausf H (variants A to H) in 1944 the volume depicts how these invincible machines were not only adapted and up-gunned to face the ever-increasing enemy threat, but were repainted and transformed in order to blend in with the local surroundings to maximize concealment.

The book also covers all different types and examples of markings on the PzKpfw IV used by various formations and tank units. The markings displayed on these vehicles gained distinction on the battlefield and evolved over the years, and a number of such changes, both of design and application, are illustrated in these pages.

During the German rearmament programme of the 1930s this account highlights how few markings on the tanks were used, but as German military increased in size and complexity during the run-up to war, colours and systems of markings on the tanks were slowly adapted and changed. National insignia, tactical numbers, markings to identify the vehicle and sub-unit at a distance plus formation and/or unit insignia were added.

The variations of the colour schemes markings of the PzKpfw IV therefore ev too throughout this volume. Some des or methods of application to these ta were changed as the war progressed. A number of divisions were ordered to change or even remove their insignia to disguise battlefield movement, especially prior to an offensive, and in some units the change became permanent. Others repainted their insignia following a battle or a protracted advance or retreat, or even repainted different styles, some of which were unofficial. Photographs in this book suggest that the change in tactical development might cause a certain amount of confusion for the reader. With a plethora of vehicles in the field not carrying markings or insignia, it is sometimes impossible to identify the area where the tank was operating. Nevertheless, it is believed that the imagery in these pages provides a useful overview of the history of the PzKpfw IV at war, the type of armament that was used, the marking practices, and the various camouflage and *zimmerit* that were applied.

The basic camouflage colours adapted before and during the war years were not extensive, but the variations seen in the field were quite considerable. During the early years of the war the standard camouflage colour was overall grey and green, and this continued into the first four months of the campaign in Russia in 1941 where the PzKpfw IV blended well on the vehicle. The PzKpfw IV became the most popular Panzer of the war, and remained in production throughout. At first it was not intended to be the main armoured vehicle of the Panzerwaffe, but it soon proved to be so diverse and effective that it became the most widely used of all the main battle tanks during the conflict.

A knocked-out Ausf E has been recovered from the battlefield and is being transported on a special low-loader vehicle to be repaired. Only the first 6 of the tactical number can be made out; the second digit, painted over the turret side door, seems to have been effaced and repainted at some point.

An Ausf H supporting an infantry drive through a Russian town during a withdrawal operation in 1944. The vehicle is painted in dark yellow RAL 7028 with a hard-edge camouflage scheme of red-brown RAL 8017 and olive green RAL 6003 stripes. Painted in white on the side of the turret skirts is 311.

to limited supplies many tanks roamed the white arctic wilderness with no camouflage at all, still retaining their standard dark grey scheme.

Photographs in this book outline how crews adapted and learnt the lessons of camouflage for survival. For this reason many crews began utilizing and adding to their camouflage schemes by finding various substitutes and applying them to the surface of their vehicles in order to break up their distinctive shapes and allow them to blend into the local terrain. By mid-war, there was a universal change to a three-colour camouflage paint system when units and even individual crews were responsible for their application.

Survival for these tank men was paramount, and the images in this new volume are testimony to that. For this reason alone the book is an invaluable source that illustrates the importance of the development, the success and the final destruction of one of the most popular Panzers in Hitler's once mighty Panzerwaffe.

with the local terrain. However, with the continued war against the Soviet Union the Panzerwaffe was compelled to apply various winter white camouflage schemes to as many vehicles as possible. But due

Origins

The origins of the Panzerkampfwagen IV (PzKpfw IV) began in the 1930s, formulated by the Panzer commander General Heinz Guderian. He conceived that he wanted a tank that would be used on the battlefield in a supporting role and used primarily against anti-tank guns and fortifications; to achieve tactical dominance against the enemy and threaten his lines a Panzer division would comprise of a medium tank, notably a PzKpfw III, and a heavier tank called a PzKpfw IV.

In January 1934, specifications were issued for the production of a medium tank, known as the PzKpfw III. To support this vehicle a short-barrelled 7.5cm heavy tank went into development, named Begleitwagen (accompanying vehicle) or BW. The name was perceived in order to disguise the vehicle's actual purpose, due to the stringent rearmament restrictions imposed on the Wermacht under the Treaty of Versailles. Rheinmetall-Borsig, Krupp and MAN each developed prototypes, but it was Krupp's vehicle that was selected for further development.

Krupp designed a tank that was known as the first model or *Ausführung* A (abbreviated to Ausf A, meaning Variant A). It was armed with a short-barrelled howitzer-type 7.5cm gun, and for local defence armed with two machine guns. The weight of the vehicle was 18 tons, with a simple leaf-spring double-bogie suspension and eight rubber-rimmed

interleaved road wheels added on either side of the chassis.

The hull comprised a 12-cylinder Maybach HL 108 TR 300 horsepower engine with twin carburettors, which was housed in the rear of the vehicle, but slightly to the right. This allowed the torque shaft to clear the rotary base junction, which gave power to rotate the turret, while linking to the transmission box mounted in the hull.

The design of the superstructure of the tank was for a five-man crew comprising the tank commander who was seated beneath the roof hatch, while his gunner was situated to the left of the gun breech and the loader positioned to the right. The driver and the radio operator sat front-left and front-right.

The frontal armour of the tank was reinforced inside the vehicle to protect the crew by cross members, steps and braces. The superstructure sides of the chassis extended out over the hull and allowed space for ammunition and equipment storage.

In order to allow the crew visual contact, special vision ports were cut out in the front wall of the chassis and the driver's vision port was protected by a thick-plated visor; two hatches were housed in the superstructure roof above the radio driver and radio operator positions. Both the radio operator and driver were also tasked with manning the MG34 machine gun.

In a victory parade in Komotau, Austria during the Anchluss on 9 October 1938 a PzKpfw IV Ausf B moves along a road much to the jubilation of the crowd lining its way. The vehicle's superstructure is painted in overall dark factory standard grey. A tactical number painted in white on the turret can just be seen, but is unidentifiable.

By 30 September 1939, 211 of these Panzerkampfwagen IVs or Versuchskraftfahrzeug 622s (VsKfz 622) had been manufactured. During this period the tank was further modified and ranged from the next variant, Ausf B, through to Ausf E. All were armed with the short 7.5cm tank gun and an MG34 in the turret. However, there were slight modifications. After Krupp had manufactured 35 tanks of the Ausf A variant, in 1937 production moved to the Ausf B. In the Ausf B the factory replaced the original engine with a more powerful 300 PS Maybach HL 120TR, and an SSG 75 transmission was installed, with six forward gears and one reverse gear. The vehicle's glacis plate was strengthened to 30mm, while the driver's visor was installed on the hull front plate, and the hull-mounted 7.92mm (0.31 in) MG34 machine gun port was replaced by a covered pistol port and visor plate. A new and modified commander's cupola hatch was produced taken from the PzKpfw III Ausf C variant with bolt-on armour. The superstructure ammunition store was reduced to save additional weight. Other modifications comprised the *nebelkerzenabwurfvorrichtung* (smoke grenade discharger rack) which was installed on the rear of the hull.

By mid-August 1938 some 42 PzKpfw IV Bs had come off the production line. During this period, the Ausf C was produced and again further modifications were made. This saw the vehicle's protection upgraded with the turret armour increased to 30mm, and the engine replaced with the powerful HL 120TRM. The radio operator in both the Ausf B and C was installed with two vision ports and a pistol port. The last Ausf Cs came off the assembly lines in August 1939 with 140 of them being produced. That same month production of the Ausf D commenced and 248 tanks were manufactured. As with

the Ausf B and C the armour thickness was strengthened. The turret's internal gun mantlet was increased to 35mm and the armoured hull sides were widened to 20mm. The KZF2 periscope gunsight in the MG ball mount and a vision port were also installed. The tank's main armament mounted the Kampfwagenkanone 37 L/24 (KwK 37 L/24) 7.5cm (2.95 in) gun, a low-velocity gun designed to mainly to fire high-explosive shells. Against armoured targets, firing the *panzergranate* (armour-piercing shell) at 430 metres per second (1,410ft/s) the KwK 37 could penetrate 43 millimetres (1.69 in), inclined at 30° at ranges of up to 700 metres (2,300ft).

Between 1938 and 1939 the Panzer regiments were supplied with these PzKpfw IV variants at a modest production rate, and 211 of them would be in the army inventory for testing in the east against Poland in September 1939. Just prior

A new PzKpfw IV Ausf D has just been delivered and is being looked over by its new crew. The Panzer retains its factory colour of dark grey RAL 7021. Painted on the side in white is its tactical number 301. Next to the tactical number is the standard Balkenkreuz painted in black with white outline.

An Ausf D displaying an improved MG ball mount, the Kugelblende 30, and a new 35mm thick external mantlet. The ventilation grilles on the side of the engine deck have also been redesigned. The tactical number 811 is painted in white on a black rhomboid plate on the hull side with a while line below, which possibly indicates that vehicle belongs to 11th Panzer Regiment of the 1st Panzer Division.

to the campaign the Panzerwaffe issued a new organization chart in which each Panzer regiment was to have two medium companies, each of which was to have two PzKpfw IVs in the HQ company, five PzKpfw IIs in one company and 12 PzKpfw IVs in three platoons of four, making a total of 14 PzKpfw IVs per company. A month later the PzKpfw IV was ready for action.

For this action the PzKpfw IV was designed purely as an infantry-support tank, and not intended to engage enemy armour, but to thrust forward, smashing through enemy defences and protecting the infantry in close support.

Blitzkrieg Years

Early War Variants

For the invasion of Poland the PzKpfw IV finally made its debut on the battlefield. The main variants used for this action were the later Ausf C and Ausf D models. Painted in their overall dark grey RAL 7021 factory finish paint and often carrying the stencilled Balkenkreuz (national cross) in solid white on the side of the turret with white-painted tactical numbers, 211 of these vehicles were divided among the five army groups that were ordered to invade Poland. The 1st and 2nd Panzer regiments each had 28 PzKpfw IVs, giving the 1st Panzer Division 56 tanks, while the 11th Panzer Regiment of the 1st Light Division also had 28 PzKpfw IVs, while the 65th Panzer Battalion had 14, for a total of 42 tanks.

During the early hours of 1 September 1939, the German army crossed the Polish frontier and so began Operation White, the codename for German invasion of Poland. Almost immediately both the Wehrmacht, Luftwaffe and Panzerwaffe quickly began achieving their objectives. The entire German thrust was swift: the devastatingly efficient blitzkrieg had arrived.

Although the Panzerwaffe was successful on all fronts, the bulk of the armoured strength was made up of the PzKpfw IIs, and because both armoured strategy and tactics were still in an experimental stage, great onus was put on the heaviest tank on the battlefield, the PzKpfw IV. Over the coming days and weeks the PzKpfw IV showed its worth on the battlefield, but at a cost. Around Warsaw the 4th Panzer

Division saw a number of heavy enemy actions trying to penetrate the Polish capital. As a result, the division lost 57 out of 120 Panzers engaged in the fighting with the loss of some of its PzKpfw IVs. However, the division went on to engage Polish formations near the city near the Bzura, employing a number of PzKpfw IVs against strong enemy resistance.

A close-up view of the crew of a PzKpfw IV. Note the divisional markings painted (in yellow) on the side of the tank. This indicated that this tank belongs to the 5th Panzer Division. No divisional signs were used in Poland, but in France the symbol was identified as an inverted Y with one round dot. In late September the division lost the 15th Panzer Regiment that was moved to the 11th Panzer Division. The division saw service in the Balkans, using the new symbol of one yellow X. The 5th Panzer Division then saw service on the Eastern Front. The 31st Panser Regiment adopted the red devil's head as a regimental symbol. This emblem, together with the yellow X was used until the end of the war.

In spite of the losses in and around Warsaw the PzKpfw IV was very successful in almost all its engagements against the enemy. Poland was its baptism of fire and although 71 tanks were lost in combat, including the loss of 19 PzKpfw IVs, the vehicle had undertaken first-rate service supporting the infantry.

Following victory in Poland, it was decided that production of the PzKpfw IV should be increased following what the Germans called 'successful troop testing'. *Neeresverordnungsblatt* (Army Instruction Sheet) 1939 No. 685 outlined that the Panzerkampfwagen IV (7.5cm SdKfz 161) was ready to be scaled up for production.

Whilst the tank production industry began stockpiling new tanks and rearming the Panzer regiments with notably the PzKpfw III and IV, the German high command was once again planning another campaign, this time in the west.

When that war was finally unleashed against the Low Countries and France in May 1940, the Panzer divisions had some 278 PzKpfw IVs available for action.

In total there were 2,072 Panzers brought to the front in the west. The 1st, 2nd and 10th Panzer divisions each had 56 PzKpfw IVs; the 6th, 7th and 8th each had 36; and the 3rd, 4th and 5th division had 24 each.

Throughout the Western campaign the PzKpfw IV fought with distinction, and supported the infantry widely throughout with little interference to the fast-moving mobile operations.

By the end of the campaign it was recognized that the PzKpfw IV would be used predominantly on the battlefield to penetrate enemy positions and support the infantry in a number of offensive roles.

As a result of its achievements from June to September 1940, Panzerwaffe inventory rose steadily from 4,150 to 4,833. On 20 August 1940 Hitler ordered that the Panzerwagen III and IV and the Panzerbefehlswagen (armoured command vehicle) be raised to a 'special level' and to increase production dramatically.

With looming plans to unleash Operation Sealion, the planned invasion of the British Isles, some 180 underwater tanks were ordered built by Hitler. On 19 August 1940, 48 PzKpfw IVs were made available to four special Panzer units designed for waterborne operations. However, within weeks plans for the invasion of England were abandoned and the Panzerwaffe began drawing up new models of the PzKpfw IV to supersede those already in service. As a direct result of this, the Krupp factory built in October 1940 the Ausf E variant. This new model had thicker 30mm armour bolted on the bow plate, and appliqué steel plates added to the glacis. A new driver's visor taken from the Sturmgeschutz III (StuG III) was added along with the commander's cupola, which was adopted from the Panzer III Ausf G and installed forward of the turret. To develop the range

and increase the number of newer models, older variants were retrofitted with these modifications when they were recalled for servicing. Some 206 Ausf Es were produced between October 1940 and April 1941.

Whilst the Ausf Es were coming off the production line, during this period the new Ausf F was produced in Magdeburg from April 1941 through to March 1942 with chassis numbers 82001–82395. This

Top: A PzKpfw IV at a depot with crew and infantry onboard. Between 1936 and 1945, over 8,000 Panzer IVs were built.

Above: Two PzKpfw IVs ford a river during operations on the Western Front in 1940. Both vehicles retain the factory colour of dark grey RAL 7021.

Left: On the Western Front a PzKpfw IV Ausf C in a field. It is painted in overall dark factory grey. As for its design, the vehicle was very similar to the Ausf B type, but can be differentiated by the armoured sleeve for the co-axial MG34 on the internal gun mantle.

An Ausf D moving along a road. This vehicle has a non-standard stowage locker fitted midway along the port-side track guard, which appears to have had its Balkenkreuz national insignia overpainted. Note: to provide additional cooling for the brakes and final drives, both hatch lids have been opened on the glacis plate.

A PzKpfw IV. Commanders in the field soon realized that only the 7.5cm gun of the PzKpfw IV was really suited to the demands of the modern battlefield. However, even this gun had its limitations. The short barrel gave the shells limited velocity, which was effective against thinly built enemy tanks but proved far from adequate against heavier tanks.

A PzKpfw IV advances through a French town during operations in May 1940. The vehicle's intended role, especially during the early part of the war, was purely as infantry support.

A commander stands up in the cupola of his PzKpfw IV. He has on the standard black Panzer uniform with the newly introduced Panzer enlisted man's field cap. He has the tank crew headset, in conjunction with a throat microphone: essential pieces of kit if the crew were to hear his orders over the engine noise.

A column of Pz Kpfw.IVs during operations on the Western Front. The PzKpfw IV fought with distinction, and supported the infantry throughout with little hindrance to the fast-moving mobile operations.

A side view of an Ausf D with the side hatch open. The commander's cupola hatch is also open. The cupola was bolted to the turret rear, which consisted of a cylindrical mantle, five upper and five lower sliding shutters, an internal azimuth indicator ring and a two-piece hatch cover.

variant was strengthened with 50mm single plate armour on the turret and hull. The main engine exhaust muffler was shortened and an auxiliary generator muffler was installed to its left. The tracks of the vehicle were wider too, and the idler wheels were changed. Instead of cast steel, two wheels were made of 60mm steel tubes welded together linked by seven welded spokes. In addition, the two maintenance hatches on the glacis that provided access to the steering brakes were now equipped with a ventilator cowl to prevent them overheating.

The Ausf F retained the effective and often deadly KwK L/24 short-barrelled gun, and 80 rounds of ammunition on board was more than enough to service the crew whilst engaged in battle.

When Barbarossa, the codename of the invasion of Russia, commenced on 22 June 1941, 64 Ausf Fs were in service. By July, a total of 531 PzKpfw IVs had been produced. The expansion of tank production grew rapidly with the onset of hostilities on the Eastern Front. Massive concentration was made on the production of the PzKpfw IV in a drastic measure to ensure that Germany would win its campaign in the East before the onset of the Russian winter.

Two photographs taken in sequence showing a PzKpfw IV in 1940. The vehicle is painted in its standard dark grey RAL 7021.

On the Eastern Front

Two PzKpfw IVs on a flatbed railway car destined for the front lines on the Eastern Front in June 1941. In the middle of the IVs is a PzKpfw I. The tank with tactical number 802 is painted in red with a black and white Balkenkreuz national insignia on the superstructure side. Camouflage scheme are the two-tone system of dark grey RAL 7021. This is over-sprayed with dark brown RAL 7017 in patches, so it covered roughly a third of the vehicle's chassis.

An Ausf D speeds past a knocked-out Russian 37mm Model 1939 anti-aircraft gun. This Panzer has been retrofitted with a stowage bin on the rear face of the turret, while the crew have stowed the additional road wheels on the track guards.

Mid War Variants

For the invasion of Russia some 439 PzKpfw IVs were made available for action in June 1941. Along a 1000-mile front, the Panzer divisions exploited the terrain in a concerted series of severe hammer blows to the Red Army. Yet the Panzer divisions were thinly spread out. Although the armoured spearheads were still achieving rapid victories on all fronts, supporting units were not keeping pace with them. Consequently, it became increasingly difficult to keep the Panzers supplied and fuelled. Nevertheless, between June and late September 1941, the Panzer and motorized divisions were more or less unhindered by lack of supply, difficult terrain or bad weather conditions. Its tanks, notably the PzKpfw IV, performed well against the T-34 and dominated lighter Soviet armour. But the Panzerwaffe lost the chance of victory in Russia as much of its arsenal was based on the mobility of wheeled instead of tracked vehicles. As a consequence, muddy roads and then snow hampered operations, grinding the German war machine to a halt.

During the long winter the Panzerwaffe was worn down by attrition, and the prospect of winning the war in Russia in 1941 was lost altogether. With massive losses sustained in the wasteland of the Soviet Union, German tank production continued with vigour to try and supplement the losses.

When the bad weather finally lifted it was not just tank production that had become a problem, it was firepower to deal with the increasing threat of heavier enemy tanks

Right: An Ausf D with tampon covering the 7.5cm KwK's gun tube. On the left mudguard, the letter K in yellow indicates that the tank belongs to Panzergruppe Kleist. The track links attached to the front of the tank are for additional armoured protection.

Far right: An Ausf D Tauchpanzer is identifiable by its modified 'non-return' exhaust pipes. 48 were converted in 1940 for the invasion of Britain, but were used in the Soviet Union. This vehicle is towing a fuel trailer (SdAh) which mounts two 200-litre drums.

A dramatic night-time image of an Ausf F1 the moment its short-barrelled 7.5cm L/24 gun is fired. The blast allows us to make out on the top left corner of its front superstructure plate, the new official 1st Panzer Division sign of a yellow inverted Y. The white turret number 821 indicates No. 1 tank, 2nd Platoon, 8th Company of the 11th Battalion, 1st Panzer Regiment.

Various PzKpfw IV variants can be seen outside the Kraftwagenhall of the 1st Squadron, 11th Cavalry Rifle Regiment, the unit that formed 24th Panzer Division in November 1941. The nearest Panzer is an Ausf E, while the next two are Ausf Bs or Cs. All are painted in overall dark grey.

An Ausf D from one of the Gruppe von Kleist Panzer divisions in the summer of 1941. This vehicle has been fitted with special jerry can racks on the roof turret and carries a number of jerry cans. The tactical number 423 can be seen painted in white on the turret side.

A Tauchpanzer IV amphibious tank on the advance. Note the absence of the usual cylindrical exhaust muffler which was fitted to non-amphibious vehicles.

An Ausf E stationary in a field during the invasion of the Soviet Union in 1941. This tank bears the two-digital tactical number 18 in yellow on the turret side and rare stowage box. Since no platoon had eight tanks this cannot be a zug-and-panzer (platoon and tank) number, and its exact significance is unclear.

An Ausf D during its drive eastward. An infantry soldier on a bicycle passes the stationary tank. A typical new Panzer division in 1941 comprised one tank regiment of two, sometimes three, *abteilungen* (battalions) totalling some 150–200 tanks, two motorized rifle (*schützen*) regiments, each of two battalions, whose infantry were carried in armoured halftracks or similar vehicles, and a reconnaissance battalion of three companies (one motorcycle, two armoured car).

A number of PzKpfw IV variants all painted in their standard grey colour, with no markings and displaying just the white-outline Balkenkreuz.

A close-up shot of an Ausf D variant stationary during a lull in the fighting in the summer of 1941. Note the Notek black-out driving headlamp positioned on the right of the vehicle.

An Ausf E in the Ukraine in 1941. This variant is identifiable by the new driver's visor, adopted from the StuG III and installed on the hull front plate. It also includes a commander's cupola, from the Panzer III Ausf G, relocated forward on the turret.

such as the T-34 medium and KV-1 heavy tanks. Plans had already been on the table before the German invasion of Russia to improve the PzKpfw IV's main armament.

By early 1942 Krupp was already in the development stages of the tank being fitted with a long 7.5cm KwK 40 gun. It was at this stage in the tank's redevelopment that designers re-designated the vehicle with the short barrel as an Ausf 1, while the longer guns bore the designation Ausf 2. The first Ausf F2 was completed in March 1942. Further development saw the production of the 7.5cm KwK 40 L/43. Production of these vehicles began in the summer of 1942 when they were converted to the Ausf G model. The design of the 7.5cm KwK40 L/43 meant that the cannon was more powerful than its short-barrelled Ausf 1 predecessor. The vehicle was fitted with additional armour plating. A double-chambered muzzle was also produced.

From June 1942, it was ordered that all PzKpfw IVs recovered from the battlefield for repair were to be rearmed with the 7.5cm KwK40. In 1942 alone some 994 PzKpfw IVs were built. By January 1943 production of the PzKpfw IV was raised from 50 to 70 vehicles a month. At the same time various modifications were made

that included 80mm frontal armour, the removal of the side turret and the loader's forward vision port in the turret, while the two racks for the spare road wheels were installed on the track guard on the left side of the hull. The ventilation system too was adapted by creating breathing slits over the engine deck on the rear of the vehicle. A new Notek headlamp also replaced the original and the signal port was removed.

On 6 March, a further addition included bolting side skirts, or *schürzen*, either side of the vehicle to protect the tank's wheels from shell fire. A new cupola hatch too was built and added to the vehicle which replaced the late variant Ausf G double-hatch cupola. In addition to this the KwK40 L/43 was replaced by the longer 7.5cm (2.95 in) KwK L/48 gun, which included a redesigned multi-baffle muzzle brake with an improved recoil.

By April 1943, Hitler declared that the PzKpfw IV should be given top priority for all-out tank production. This also included yet again another variant, the Ausf H. This new model was built at three assembly facilities. Whilst the majority of the chassis were produced as tanks with turrets and superstructures, some of the chassis were diverted to assembly plants to construct the Sturmgeschütz IV and the Sturmpanzer IV.

Production of the Ausf H was rushed onto the assembly lines in June 1943 before the planned summer offensive in Russia commenced. The model was born out of the necessity to replace heavy losses, so the vehicle was greatly simplified to speed production. The tank had improved single 80mm glacis armour bolted to the vehicle. The turret roof and segments of the chassis and hull sides were reinforced too. The vehicle also received an application of *zimmerit* anti-magnetic mine paste over the chassis and *schürzen*.

Whilst the PzKpfw IV had been coming off the assembly lines, other vehicles in the Panzerwaffe arsenal too had been building up strength in the badly depleted Panzer divisions. By the summer they fielded some 24 Panzer divisions on the Eastern Front alone. This was a staggering transformation of a Panzer force that had lost immeasurable amounts of armour in less than two years of combat. Now, with this force, Hitler intended to risk his precious Panzerwaffe in what became the largest tank battle of the Second World War, at Kursk, codenamed, Operation Zitadelle (Citadel).

Two stationary PzKpfw IVs on a road in the Soviet Union. They are both painted in dark grey RAL 7021 and carry large red with white outlined tactical numbers on the rear of the stowage bin. A standard black and white Balkenkreuz is seen painted on the rear of the leading tank.

A column of PzKpfw IVs moving towards the front in the winter of 1941. None of these vehicles has received any application of winter whitewash and they still retain their distinctive standard grey painted finish RAL 7021.

During winter operations an Ausf J has received a very liberal coat of whitewash on its chassis.

A whitewashed PzKpfw IV during the winter of 1941. This vehicle has received quite an extensive winter whitewash, but often during this first winter in Russia there was a shortage of white camouflage paint. This regularly led to improvisations, such as dense scribbles of chalk applied to the dark grey chassis.

A PzKpfw IV is well concealed in the winter vegetation during operations in Russia. The brown and white terrain blends with the grey and partly whitewashed tank.

An up-gunned and up-armoured PzKpfw IV Ausf F during the summer of 1942 on what appears to be a training ground. Next to it stands a PzKpfw III Ausf L.

An Ausf G partially enters the water along an estuary in the summer of 1942. The light colour of the vehicle suggests that it is also painted in a tropical scheme, which was quite common for Panzers during this period, especially in southern Russia.

An Ausf G being towed out of the mud by another PzKpfw IV. The tank mounts a Bosch black-out headlamp on both fenders. It mounts the long 7.5cm KwK L/48 and road antenna. Note the candle smoke dischargers installed on the turret side.

An up-gunned and up-armoured Ausf F during 1942. Next to it is a PzKpfw III Ausf L.

The crew of an Ausf G in the summer of 1942.

A column of PzKpfw IVs advances across the Russian steppe. The near vehicle is an Ausf G and mounts the powerful long-barrelled 7.5cm KwK. However, interestingly, it has no tray for the spare road wheels on the port-side fender, has no mounted Bosch headlamp, and retains the split cupola hatch lid. This indicates the Panzer was most probably a former Ausf 2.

Kursk and Beyond

A column of PzKpfw IVs during operations in North Africa. The vehicles have been painted in the new tropical paint scheme consisting of two-thirds yellow brown RAL 8000 and one-third grey green RAL 7008.

A stationary PzKpfw IV with crew in a field. It is painted in overall dark yellow RAL 7028 and markings are limited to a standard black Balkenkreuz painted on the side.

Late War Variants

For Operation Zitadelle the Panzerwaffe was able to muster in early July 17 divisions and two brigades with no less than 1,715 Panzers and 147 Sturmegeschutz III assault guns. Each division averaged some 98 Panzers and self-propelled anti-tank guns.

Putting together such a strong force was a great achievement, but the Panzerwaffe of 1943 was unlike those armoured forces that had victoriously steamrolled across western Russia two years earlier. The losses during the previous winter had resulted in the drastic reductions in troop strength. Despite the Panzerwaffe's impressive array

of firepower, this shortage of infantry was to lead to Panzer units being required to take on more ambitious tasks normally reserved for the infantry. As a result of the shortages much of the effort fell to the 841 PzKpfw IVs. This was a massive undertaking, especially against strong Russian defences.

Initially the Panzerwaffe fared well, but through sheer weight of Soviet strength and stubborn combat along an ever-extending front, German mobile units were soon forced to a standstill. The losses that the Panzerwaffe sustained at Kursk were so immense that it led to the Wermacht taking its first steps of the inexorable retreat back to Germany. The Russians had managed to destroy no less than 30 divisions, seven of which were Panzer. German reinforcements were insufficient to replace the staggering losses, so they fought on understrength. The Panzers were now duty-bound to improvise with what they had at their disposal and to try and maintain themselves in the field, and in doing so they hoped to wear down the enemy's offensive capacity.

In other areas of the Russian front the situation was just as dire. The Panzerwaffe had no other choice than to fight on mercilessly whilst simultaneously the production lines worked on at full capacity trying to replace the significant numbers lost in the summer campaign. In October and November 1943 only five Panzer divisions and one SS Panzer division were sent as replacements to the Eastern Front.

Between October 1943 and September 1944 a total of 1,148 PzKpfw IVs and Sturmgeschutz IVs were delivered to the front. This was a massive shortfall, and it was not enough to replace those already being damaged or lost. In October 1943, 73 were produced, with the loss of over 100, and in November 50 came off the assembly lines, followed in December by 52. The shortfall in the PzKpfw IV was so immense that it often fell to assault guns like the StuG III to support the lines.

In total for 1943, some 816 PzKpfw IVs were manufactured. By early 1944, in a bid to increase the firepower of the PzKpfw IV, the final version of the tank, known as the Ausf J variant, went into production. This model was produced through to the end of the war.

Once again there were various modifications to improve the vehicle's battlefield survivability. The turret, which was electrically powered, was removed so that it could be moved manually. This not only allowed quick hand operation to traverse the turret, but also allowed more space to install an additional 200-litre fuel tank which increased the tank's road range to 200 miles. Other alterations consisted of removing the vision and pistol ports on the turret side hatches, modification of the radiator, increasing the armour on the turret roof and replacing the cylindrical mufflers by two flame-suppressing mufflers. In order to try and reduce weight and the cost of manufacture, the vehicle's *schürzen* were replaced by wire mesh. The application of *zimmerit* anti-magnetic mine paste too was no longer applied, and the gunner's forward vision port was removed. There were other smaller alterations undertaken to reduce cost and further increase production.

In spite of the Panzerwaffe's drastic measures to manufacture and improve the PzKpfw IV, nothing would impede the relentless Soviet offensive westward. By mid-1944 the Panzerwaffe was frantically trying to hold the receding front. Yet in spite of the constant military setbacks, confidence was bolstered by the efforts of the armaments industry as they begun producing many new vehicles for the Eastern Front. In fact, during 1944, the Panzerwaffe was better supplied with equipment during any other time on the Eastern Front, thanks to Herr Speer's armaments industry. In total some 20,000 fighting vehicles including 8,328 medium and heavy tanks, 5,751 assault guns, 3,617 tank destroyers and 1,246 self-propelled artillery carriages of various types reached the Eastern Front. Included in these new arrivals was the second generation of tank-destroyers such as the Jagdpanzer IV. In fact, tank-destroyers and assault guns would soon outnumber the tanks, which was confirmation of the Panzerwaffe's obligation to performing a defensive role against overwhelming opposition. However, all of these vehicles found themselves irrevocably stretched along a very thin and fragile front, with many of them rarely reaching the proper operating level. With too few of them delivered, Panzer crews soon found themselves unable to make any considerable dent against the growing tank might of the Red Army. What followed during the last months of 1944 was a frantic attempt by the Panzerwaffe to stem the Soviet drive through Poland.

Whilst tank crews tried in vain to hold back the Russian advance the armament factories were being bombed by the Allies, further reducing tank output. On 17 October 1944, a heavy air attack struck the Nibelungenwerke, severely hindering production of the PzKpfw IV.

By early 1945 the Allied air offensive had caused so much damage to tank-manufacturing centres that production had fallen to pre-1942 levels, with only around 55 tanks per month coming off the assembly lines.

As a consequence to the bombing campaign, and the overwhelming losses on both battle fronts, east and west, the Panzerwaffe no longer had the manpower, war plant or transportation to accomplish

A PzKpfw IV halted in a field. The vehicle is finished in a summer camouflage scheme of dark yellow RAL 7028 with over-sprayed patches of olive green RAL 6003. The tactical number 612 has been stencilled in white on the spaced armour plates on the turret side.

Images of a late variant PzKpfw IV seen during the summer offensive at Kursk in July 1943. The tactical number 420 can clearly be seen on its spaced turret plates. Painted next to the tactical numbers is divisional insignia of the 'Berlin bear', always associated with the 3rd Panzer Division. Yet the frontal photo shows equally the yellow Yr or 'man rune' of the 4th Panzer Division, left of the MG34 machine gun port. From divisional records its noted from 1943 the 6th Regiment of the 3rd Panzer Division bore an extra marking – a black shield with the 4th Panzer Division rune above crossed swords in yellow. This suggests that men transferred from the 4th to the 3rd Panzer Division were commemorating their old unit.

An Ausf G during the Italian campaign. The vehicle is commonly painted in overall dark yellow RAL 7028. Wrapped around the 7.5cm gun tube is fixed camouflage of what appears to be dried straw. Fixed camouflage was used throughout the war to often conceal a tank or self-propelled artillery occupying a fixed position.

Two Ausf Hs, as identified by the additional bolted 30mm appliqué armour. Both vehicles are painted in solid dark yellow, although the 7.5cm gun tubes appear to be in a darker shade, possibly red-oxide primer, which was used as a basecoat.

An Ausf J on the Eastern front in the summer of 1944. This Panzer was the final variant that went into production in 1944. This vehicle was modified by removal of the pistol and vision ports in the turret, and the engine's radiator housing was simplified by changing the slanted sides to straight sides. Due to the lack of steel the vehicle's side skirts were replaced by wire mesh. However, no mesh has been installed on this vehicle.

a proper build-up of forces in the defence of the Reich.

As for the PzKpfw IV, it fought on to the end in various ad hoc units, embroiled in sustained defensive actions. However, its success was limited and localized and did nothing to avert eventual defeat. But the PzKpfw IV had scored considerable successes on the battlefield. It was one of the very few vehicles in the Panzerwaffe to be produced in large numbers throughout the war; it provided the very backbone of Germany's defensive and offensive actions and although the tank never overwhelmed its enemy, its crew fought with courage and zeal to the very end.

A long column of whitewashed PzKpfw IVs during operations in the winter of 1943/44. The leading tank has track links bolted to the front of the tank and on the roof turret for additional armoured protection.

An Ausf H belonging to the infamous 12th SS Panzer Division Hitlerjugend seen here in Normandy. Initially, zimmerit was applied to the hull as well as the turret and hull schürzen plates, but here appears to be only applied to the chassis itself.

The 31st Panzer Regiment, 5th Panzer Division went into the Polish campaign partially equipped with Panzer IV Ausf Bs, marked like this example. (Tom Cooper)

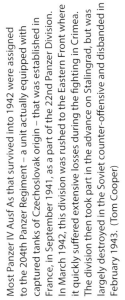

Most Panzer IV Ausf As that survived into 1942 were assigned to the 204th Panzer Regiment – a unit actually equipped with captured tanks of Czechoslovak origin – that was established in France, in September 1941, as a part of the 22nd Panzer Division. In March 1942, this division was rushed to the Eastern Front where it quickly suffered extensive losses during the fighting in Crimea. The division then took part in the advance on Stalingrad, but was largely destroyed in the Soviet counter-offensive and disbanded in February 1943. (Tom Cooper)

Prior to the invasion of Poland, all German armoured vehicles were marked with large white crosses for identification purposes. However, these proved excellent targets for Polish gunners and were thus hurriedly covered with whatever dark colour, or at least mud, was available. These two Panzer IV Ausf As served with the 1st Panzer Regiment, 1st Panzer Division during the Polish campaign. (Tom Cooper)

Three early variants of the Panzer IV were available at the start of the Second World War: Ausfs A, B and C. This example is an Ausf B of the 11th Panzer Regiment, 6th Panzer Division, on exercise in western Germany in early 1940, just prior to the invasion of France. It wears no turret insignia on top of its base coat of dark grey (dunkelgrau), also Panzergrau RAL 7021. The tactical number is applied in white on the number plate attached to the side of the hull instead, right next to the Balkenkreuz outlined in white and the 6th Division's tactical insignia of an inverted Y with two yellow dots.

Tom Cooper

This Panzer IV Ausf D from the 3rd Panzer Regiment, 2nd Panzer Division participated in the French campaign of May/June 1940 while still wearing relatively simple insignia on the base coat of Panzergrau: the tactical number on the small rhomboid plate attached to the side of the superstructure, the Balkenkreuz and the tactical insignia of the 2nd Panzer Division. (Tom Cooper)

This Panzer IV Ausf E served with the 15th Panzer Regiment, 11th Panzer Division during the campaign against Yugoslavia and Greece in April 1941. Notable is the tactical insignia of the division stencilled on the front of the superstructure, but also the 'Ghost' insignia – which saw widespread use on tanks of this unit. (Tom Cooper)

Of the 17 Panzer IVs that served in Libya with the 5th Panzer Regiment, 5th Leichte Division – the original core of the Deutsches Afrikakorps – in March 1941, was this Panzer IV Ausf D, upgraded to E-like standard through the addition of the new lower commander's cupola, and 30mm armour plate around the superstructure and the hull. Originally painted in Panzergrau overall, it received a light disruptive pattern of brown RAL 8020 enhanced by a heavy coat of dust and sand. Its tactical number 800 was left as originally applied before its delivery to Africa: a simple white outline around the superstructure that identified it as the vehicle assigned to the company commander of 8th Company. It was captured by the British Eighth Army during Operation Crusader in late November 1941.

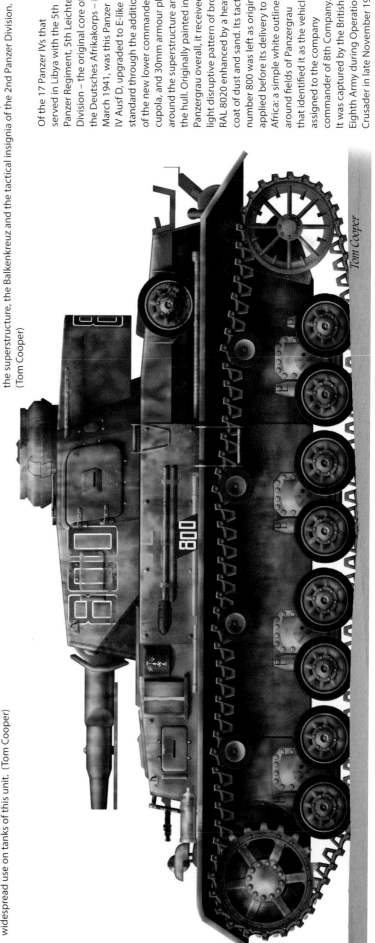

Tom Cooper

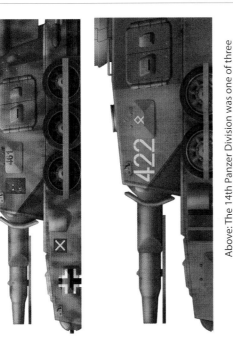

Right: This is an Ausf F1 from the 31st Panzer Regiment, 5th Panzer Division on the Eastern Front, sometime in late 1941 or early 1942. This division was originally scheduled to reinforce Rommel in North Africa, but then rushed to the USSR because of heavy losses there. Thus, it went into that war with most of its tanks camouflaged in brown RAL 8020 and grey RAL 7027. Tactical divisional insignia (a yellow X) was applied next to the Balkenkreuz, on the forward part of the superstructure, on a quadrant left in the original colour (Panzergrau). Furthermore, it received that division's *Teufel* (Devil) insignia on the turret. Typical for tanks of the 31st Panzer Regiment of that period was the application of their tactical vehicle number (461 in this case) on the visor slot on the side of the turret. (Tom Cooper)

Like tanks of the 14th Panzer Division, those of the 24th Panzer Regiment, 24th Panzer Division went into the battle for Stalingrad still painted in Panzergrau overall. Divisional insignia – in form of a leaping horse (originally the insignia of the 1st Cavalry Division, from which the 24th was established) – was usually applied on the front of the right fender. By November 1942, surviving vehicles received a coat of whitewash over their top sides, turret and the sides of the superstructure. This was the condition in which this vehicle was captured by the Russians, on the capitulation of the German pocket inside the city, on 1 March 1943. (Tom Cooper)

Above: The 14th Panzer Division was one of three armoured divisions directly involved in Operation Fall Blau (Case Blue), the advance on Stalingrad, in summer 1942. Most of its vehicles were still painted in Panzergrau overall. Their tactical numbers were applied in yellow or white, in front of the visor slot on the turret's side, which in turn was decorated with the tactical insignia for the division. This Ausf F1 was eventually knocked out by Soviet troops in the streets of Stalingrad. (Tom Cooper)

A small number of Ausf F2s – or 'Panzer IV specials' as they were known by the British – entered service in North Africa during the Battle of Gazala that culminated in the Axis capture of Tobruk, in June 1942. By August 1942, enough of them became available to equip several zugs, or platoons, of the 2nd, 7th and 8th companies of the 5th Panzer Regiment during the Axis advance into Egypt. This example survived all four battles of El Alamein, but was captured after running out of fuel during Rommel's withdrawal towards Tripoli, in November 1942.

The Grossdeutschland Motorized Infantry Division was created from the Grossdeutschland Infantry Regiment, the elite force of the Wehrmacht. By 1942, this was reinforced through the addition of the Grossdeutschland Panzer Regiment, equipped with Panzer IV Ausf Gs, among others. While most of these were left in Panzergrau overall, some received a camouflage pattern in brown RAL 8020. The Grossdeutschland Panzer Regiment used its own system for turret insignia, including one, two, or three bars and a digit, and usually applied its unit insignia (a Stahlhelm applied in white) on the right front fender of its tanks. (Tom Cooper)

Originally assigned to 66 Panzer-Kompanie zur besonderen Verwendung (66th Tank Company for Special Purposes), this Panzer IV Ausf F2 was attached to the Malta invasion force (Operation Hercules), in April 1942. In August of the same year, when that operation was cancelled, the unit in question – colloquially known as 'Kompanie Bethke' after its commander – was sent to the Eastern Front instead and integrated as the 8th Company into the 29th Panzer Regiment, 12th Panzer Division. The vehicle was painted in brown RAL 8020, red-brown (ziegelrot, lit. brick-red) RAL 8017 and green RAL 6003, and certainly wore turret markings applied in this fashion, although it is unclear if digits were applied in red and yellow.

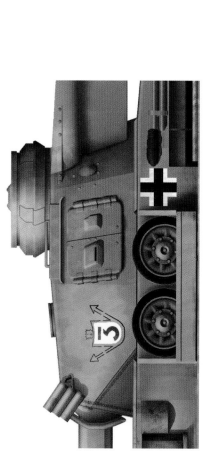

In a rush to reinforce tthe defences of Sicily, in mid-1943, the Wehrmacht marshalled its units from the various divisions that had failed to reach North Africa on time and, on 1 July 1943, established the 15th Panzergrenadier Division. This included its own armoured element, the 215th Panzer Battalion, later redesignated as the 115th Panzer Battalion. The 15th Panzergrenadier Division, which used the insignia of a white star (usually applied on the rear of the superstructure of its tanks), withdrew to the Italian mainland in August of the same year, but without this 3rd Company Panzer IV Ausf G that had been knocked out during the fighting somewhere on northern Sicily. (Tom Cooper)

Tom Cooper

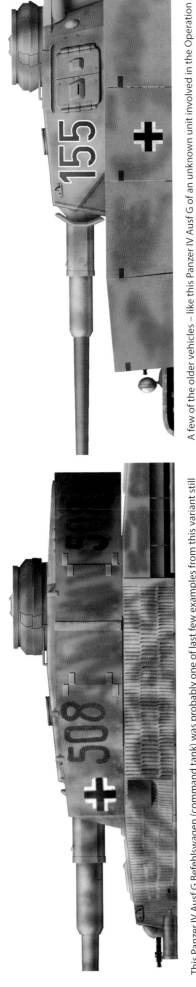

This Panzer IV Ausf G Befehlswagen (command tank) was probably one of last few examples from this variant still operational on the Eastern Front as of 1944. Notable is the application of the *zimmerit* anti-magnetic mine-paste coating on the superstructure, and *schürzen* around the turret. The camouflage consisted of the base coat of dark yellow (*dunkelgelb*) RAL 7028 oversprayed by olive-green RAL 6003 and red-brown RAL 8017. As usual for 1944, its turret number has been crudely applied by hand and brush in red-brown – and then on no less than two spots on each side of the turret skirts. (Tom Cooper)

A few of the older vehicles – like this Panzer IV Ausf G of an unknown unit involved in the Operation Zitadelle (Citadel) – went into the Battle of Kursk after receiving only the *schürzen* protecting the hull sides. As so often in 1942 and 1943, the replacement tube for its Kwk 40 L/43 was still painted in Panzergrau. (Tom Cooper)

During the course of preparations for Operation Zitadelle (Citadel), the Wehrmacht introduced a number of upgrades to its tanks. Most striking of these was the addition of *schürzen* (skirts), metal plates designed to cause premature detonation of rounds from Soviet anti-tank rifles. Further testing showed that these plates also provided effective protection from high-explosive rounds, thus *schürzen* were introduced on all Panzer IIIs and IVs still in service. This example – painted in brown RAL 8020 and olive-green – was assigned to the 2nd Panzer Division during the Battle of Kursk. Based in Vienna, Austria since 1938, its turret insignia is the Viennese coat of arms.

Tom Cooper

In reaction to disastrous losses to Allied offensives in north-western France and on the Eastern Front in the summer the 1944, the Wehrmacht scrambled to establish a number of 'Panzer brigades'. This vehicle – originally painted in brown RAL 8020 but then receiving a thick coat of olive-green RAL 6003 and some brown – is believed to have been assigned to either the 106th Panzer Brigade Feldherrnhalle or an unknown Panzergrenadier division in France in September or October 1944. Essentially little more than newly established Panzer regiments, the concept of the Panzer brigade proved a bad idea. Lacking support from such specialized formations like reconnaissance, most of these units suffered heavy losses within weeks of their deployment to the front. (Tom Cooper)

Seen in France, in April 1944, this Panzer IV Ausf H of 7th Company, 2nd Battalion of the Panzer Lehr Division was photographed during an exercise, carrying plenty of jerrycans on the top of its turret and in multiple places around the hull. As usual for vehicles of this division, it was camouflaged in brown RAL 8020 with a mottled pattern in olive green. (Tom Cooper)

Tom Cooper

The Panzer IV Ausf H entered production in June 1943, and brought a number of significant upgrades, including the longer KwK 40 L/48 gun with a redesigned multi-baffle muzzle brake, thicker front armour and commander's cupola, full *schürzen* (that resulted in the elimination of all vision ports on the hull side) and a new, stronger power wheel. This example, photographed on the Eastern Front in winter 1944, further received an almost complete coat of winter whitewash paint. Its tactical number 842 was originally painted in red with white outline, but was then re-applied in black over the whitewash by hand.

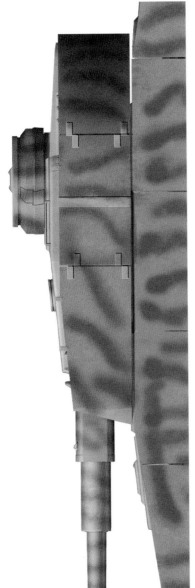

The camouflage on German tanks of 1944 was often applied in the field and in a rush. Official rations for each crew consisted of only two kilograms of a dark green colour that could be diluted with any petroleum-based liquid (or even water) and applied as a spray. Unsurprisingly, tank crews regularly made use of paints either captured from the Soviets or 'borrowed' from the Luftwaffe, and instead of broad stripes, camouflaged their vehicles in a rather haphazard fashion. This example, photographed on the Eastern Front in late summer 1944, went into battle still wearing its base coat of brown RAL 8020, and only rudely applied camouflage stripes in green, while wearing no national or tactical insignia. (Tom Cooper)

This Panzer IV Ausf H was photographed in Poland in summer 1944, while painted in dark yellow RAL 7028, olive-green RAL 6003 and red-brown RAL 8017. Probably a replacement vehicle, it went into the battle wearing no insignia other than the white outline of the Balkenkreuz applied on the side of the turret side-skirts.

Tom Cooper

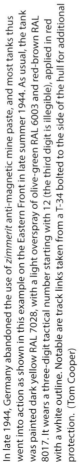

In late 1944, Germany abandoned the use of *zimmerit* anti-magnetic mine paste, and most tanks thus went into action as shown in this example on the Eastern Front in late summer 1944. As usual, the tank was painted dark yellow RAL 7028, with a light overspray of olive-green RAL 6003 and red-brown RAL 8017. It wears a three-digit tactical number starting with 12 (the third digit is illegible), applied in red with a white outline. Notable are track links taken from a T-34 bolted to the side of the hull for additional protection. (Tom Cooper)

This Panzer IV Ausf J was photographed on the Eastern Front in summer 1944. Painted in dark yellow RAL 7028, it received a light overspray of olive-green RAL 6003 and red-brown RAL 8017. The rather unusual two-digit tactical number was applied in red with a white outline on the sides and the rear of the turret skirts. Notable is the use of spare track links to improve its armoured protection. (Tom Cooper)

The final sub-variant of the Panzer IV Ausf J entered service in early 1945, and was generally considered a 'retrograde' from the Ausf H. Born of necessity to replace heavy losses, it was greatly simplified to speed up production: not only that its turret had to be rotated manually, but also all the remaining vision and pistol ports were removed. The most striking external differences were the use of three return rollers made of steel and the replacement of the side-skirts by wire mesh (only the frame for their installation is shown here). By then most vehicles were being camouflaged in the factory: while official orders demanded application of olive-green RAL 6003 and red-brown RAL 8017 to the base coat of dark yellow RAL 7028, the red primer undercoat was often left unpainted instead, with spots of green or dark yellow applied to it. This example served with the 7th Company, 31st Panzer Regiment, 5th Panzer Division in Lithuania, in early 1945.

The Panzer IV was developed into many specialized variants. One of the best known of these was the Panzerjäger IV (Sd.Kfz.162) Jagdpanzer IV/70. Based on the chassis of the Panzer IV Ausf H, this was designed as a mobile anti-tank cannon, but often deployed instead of tanks. This example has received a heavy coating of *zimmerit* anti-magnetic mine paste across the whole of the hull and superstructure, including its cast *topfblende*. It is painted in dark yellow RAL 7028, with a light overspray of olive-green (RAL 6003) and red-brown RAL 8017.

Tom Cooper

The Flakpanzerkampfwagen IV (Sd.Kfz. 161/4) or Flakpanzer IV Wirbelwind, was designed to provide air defence to armoured formations, and deployed in some numbers on the Western Front, starting in summer 1944. This example received the late-war, hard-edged camouflage pattern consisting of dark yellow RAL 7028 and olive-green RAL 6003 either applied over the red primer colour, or the red-brown RAL 8017.

Tom Cooper

PzKpfw IV Ausf D. The overall dark grey RAL 7021 factory finish is heavily powdered with pale dust. The Balkenkreuz has been stencil-painted on the superstructure side without first removing the radio antenna trough. The only visible marking is the Balkenkreuz and the three-digit tactical number stencilled on the side: 712 in white outline. The tactical number can also just be seen on the rear of the turret box.

PzKpfw IV Ausf E, Eastern Front, summer 1941. This tank bears the two-digit tactical number 18 painted in yellow on the turret side and rare stowage box. Since no platoon had eight tanks this cannot be a Zug-and-panzer number, and its exact significance is unclear. The vehicle is painted in overall factory grey RAL 7021.

PzKpfw IV Ausf H, Western Front, Normandy, 1944. The Panzer has a tactical number 13 painted on the side of the turret in white next to the standard Balkenkruez. The tank is painted in dark yellow RAL 7028 with a camouflage scheme of small red-brown RAL 8017 and large olive-green RAL 6003 patches.

Tom Cooper

PzKpfw IV Ausf A, Eastern Front, summer 1941. This Panzer with its distinctive cupola is painted in overall dark grey RAL 7021. The large tactical number 621 is painted on the turret side in white and underlined with a white strip. It also bears a large painted Balkenkruez with a white outline.

Tom Cooper

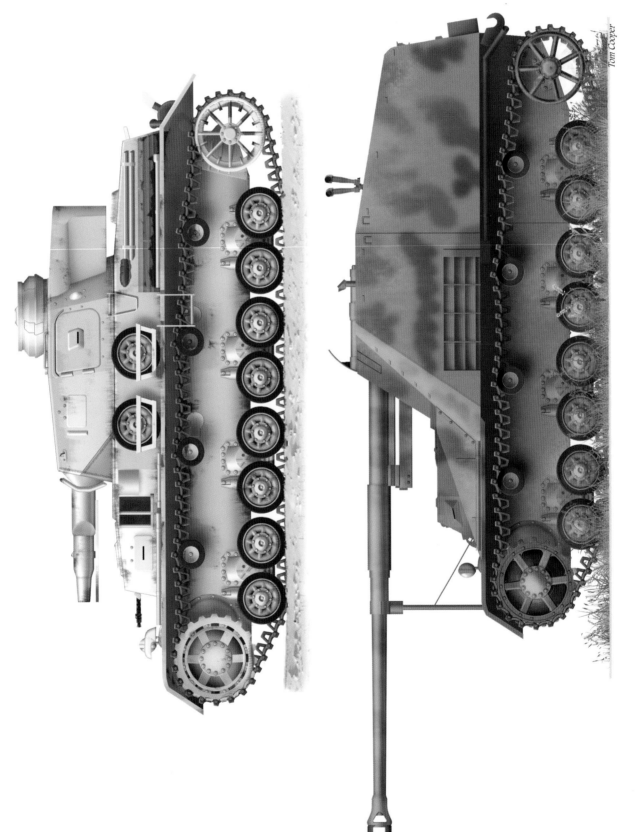

PzKpfw IV, Ausf D, Eastern Front, winter 1941. This Panzer has received an application of winter whitewash paint and no markings are visible. (Tom Cooper)

Panzerjäger Nashorn 8.8cm PaK 43 (L/71) auf Geschützwagen III/IV (SdKfz 164), Italian Front, spring 1944. This vehicle is painted in dark yellow RAL 7028 with a camouflage scheme of red-brown RAL 8017 and olive-green RAL 6003 patches. No markings are visible.

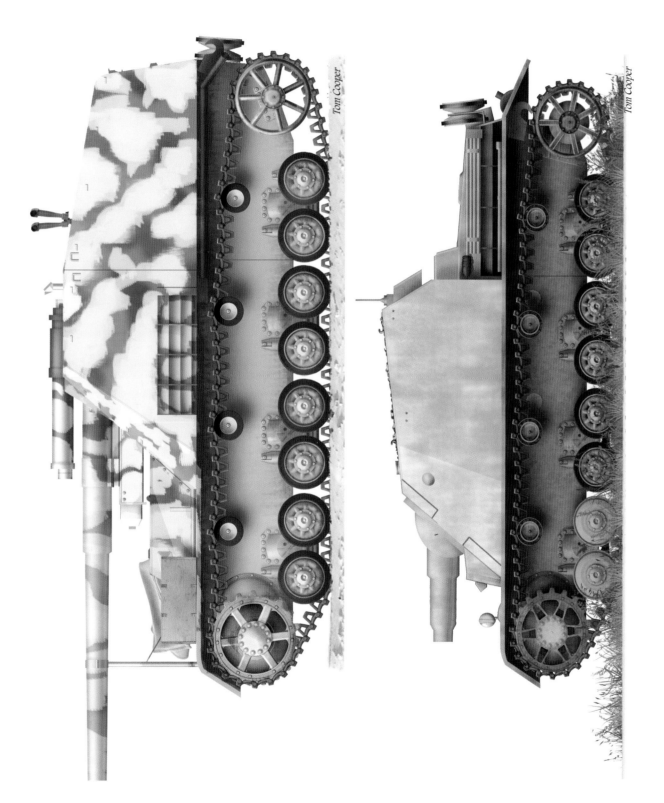

Hummel Geschützwagen III/IV sFH18/1 (SF), Eastern Front, 1943. This vehicle is painted in overall dark sand and has winter white camouflage paint scheme applied in an irregular, hard-edge pattern leaving only parts of the summer camouflage scheme of olive-green RAL 6003 and red-brown RAL 8017 visible in streaks across the hull and cannon. There are no other markings.

Sturmpanzer 43, Italian Front, summer 1944. This Sturmpanzer or Brummbar is painted in its factory coat of dark yellow RAL 7028. There are no visible markings nor has the vehicle received a coating of *zimmerit* anti-magnetic mine paste.

Flakpanzer IV Mobelwagen (SdKfz 161/3), unknown flak artillery battalion, Eastern Front, Germany, March 1945. This Mobelwagen was built on a chassis of a PzKpfw IV Ausf J. It is painted in dark yellow RAL 7028 with a camouflaged scheme of small red-brown RAL 8017 and large olive-green RAL 6003 patches. No other markings are visible except for a small Balkenkreuz painted on the side.

StuG IV, unknown unit, Russia, summer 1944. This late-production StuG IV is painted in dark yellow RAL 7028 with a hard-edge camouflage scheme of red-brown RAL 8017 and olive-green RAL 6003 stripes on its *schürzen*. The camouflage scheme appears not to have been painted on the vehicle itself which is likely the standard three-colour camouflage scheme applied with soft edges. There are no visible markings.

Tom Cooper

Tom Cooper

Camouflage and Zimmerit

Between 1939 and 1941 Panzer camouflage was fairly standardized throughout with virtually all equipment painted in dark grey. Even by the time the Germans invaded the Soviet Union the vehicles were still painted in their overall dark grey camouflage scheme, which blended well against the local terrain. However, with the drastic onset of winter and the first snow showers at the end of October 1941, Panzer crews would soon be filled with anxiety, as their vehicles were not camouflaged for winter warfare. With the worrying prospects of fighting in Russia in the snow the Wehrmacht reluctantly issued washable white winter camouflage paint in November 1941. The paint was specially designed to be thinned with water and applied to all vehicles and equipment where snow was on the ground. The application of this new winter whitewash paint could easily be washed off by the crews in the spring, exposing the dark grey base colour. Unfortunately for the crews the order came too late and the distribution to the front was delayed by weeks. Consequently, the crews had to adapt and find various crude substitutes to camouflage their vehicles. This included hastily applying their vehicles with a rough coat of lime whitewash, whilst others used lumps of chalk, white cloth strips and sheets, and even hand-packed snow in a drastic attempt to conceal conspicuous dark grey parts. Other vehicles, however, roamed the arctic steppes with no camouflage at all.

Following the harsh winter of 1941, the spring of 1942 saw the return of the dark grey base colour on all the vehicles. It was during this period that a number of vehicles saw the return of pre-war dark brown and dark green camouflage schemes. Crews had learnt from the previous year the lessons of camouflage. For this reason many crews began utilizing and adding to their camouflage schemes by finding various substitutes and applying them to the surface of the vehicle. This included the widespread use of foliage and bundles of grass and hay. This was a particularly effective method and was often used to break up the distinctive shapes and allow them to blend into the local terrain. Mud too was used as an effective form of camouflage but was never universally appreciated among the crews.

For the first time in southern Russia, in the Crimea and the Caucasus, where the summer weather is similar to that in North Africa, many vehicles were given an application of tropical camouflage, with the widespread use of sand colour schemes, almost identical to those used by the Afrika Korps. In southern Russia in the summer the terrain was very similar to that of a desert and for that reason the vehicles were completed in the tropical colours of yellow brown RAL 8000, grey green RAL 7008 or just brown RAL 8017.

By 1943, olive green was being used on vehicles, weapons and large pieces of equipment. A red-brown colour RAL 8012 had also been introduced at the same

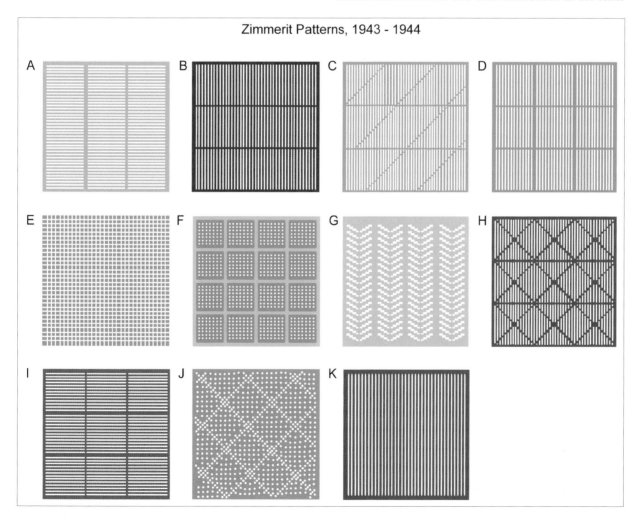

Zimmerit Patterns, 1943 - 1944

time. These two colours, along with a new colour base of dark yellow RAL 7028 were issued to crews in the form a highly concentrated paste. The paste arrived in 2kg and 20kg cans, and units were ordered to apply these cans of coloured paste over the entire surface of the vehicle. The paste was specially adapted so that it could be thinned with water or even fuel, and could be applied by spray, brush or mop.

The dark yellow paste was issued primarily to cover unwanted colours or areas of the camouflage schemes, especially during changes in seasons. These new variations of colours gave the crews the widest possible choices in schemes so as to blend in as much as possible to the local terrain. The pastes were also used to colour all canvas tops and tarpaulins on the vehicles.

The new three-colour paint scheme worked very well on the front lines and allowed each unit maximum advantage, depending on the surrounding conditions. However, within months there were frequent problems with supply. Support vehicles carrying the new paste had to travel so far to various scattered units, even from railheads, that frequently Panzer units never received any new application of camouflage schemes. Another problem was due to the fact that many Panzer units were already heavily embroiled in bitter fighting and had neither the vehicles to spare nor manpower to pull them out for a repaint. Even rear area ordnance workshops were returning vehicles to action at such speed that they only managed time to replace parts before sending them back to the front with no repaint. A great many number of vehicles never received any paste colours at all, and those that fought on remained in dark yellow, sometimes with crews adapting and enhancing the scheme with the application of foliage and mud.

However, of all the failings, the greatest of them all was actually the paints themselves. These proved to be unstable when mixed with water, and even the lightest downpour could cause these new colours to run or wash off the vehicles. Even fuel, which was used to give the paste a durable finish, was at such a premium during the later stages of the war, that units were compelled to use water, waste oil and mixed or other paints. All this caused immense variations in the appearance of the paint schemes and as a consequence there were unusual colours like brick red, chocolate brown and light green. In spite of these variations in colour and the fact that there had become little standardization in the camouflage schemes, occasionally though there were complete units that appeared on the front lines properly painted and marked. But this was often a rare occurrence, especially by 1944.

Throughout 1944, a further drain on German supplies and resources caused considerable disruption of materials. The paint system on the vehicles was just one of many hundreds of deprivations that were inflicted on the already badly depleted Panzer units. During the last months of 1944, the Panzer supply became critical and lots of vehicles were seen in overall dark yellow.

By this time almost all the new vehicles that had left the last remaining factories for the front were in their base colour dark yellow. They never received any further camouflage treatment, other than covering with foliage.

The use of foliage during the last years of the war was extensive. Most vehicles and a large range of weapons attached foliage to break up the distinctive shapes. The Germans were masters in the art of camouflaging their vehicles with branches from trees, grass and hay. In fact, some vehicles carried so much foliage that it was sometimes difficult to determine what type of vehicle they were or what camouflage scheme it had. In the last furious year of the war, foliage became more important than colour. To the crews being concealed from aerial attack it was the key to survival. As the remnants of the once-vaunted Panzer divisions withdrew across Poland to the borders of the Reich the crews did not dare waste any time painting vehicles. The widespread use of foliage helped compensate for this.

Zimmerit **Patterns**

Zimmerit was applied in a number of various patterns. A complete list of the most popular patterns that were applied to the different vehicles between 1943 and 1944 is shown on page 31. Some of the patterns were rarely ever seen.

Top: A Panzer crewman posing in summer 1944 with his Ausf G command tank. Note the *zimmerit* anti-magnetic mine paste coating on the superstructure, and the spaced armour plates around the turret. The base coat of dark yellow RAL 7028 is over-sprayed with patches of olive-green RAL 6003 and red-brown RAL 8017. The tactical number 508 has been crudely hand-painted in red-brown in two places on the turret plates; the Balkenkreuz has been applied on an uncamouflaged patch of dark yellow for better visibility.

Above: The same Panzer crewman inside an Ausf G. The frontal view shows that the turret front and mantlet have also received a non-regulation coat of *zimmerit*. This vehicle is armed the 7.5cm KwK 40L/48 gun. For local defence the Panzer is armed with an MG34 machine gun.

Panzer IV Ausf H
NORMANDY 1944
1:35 Scale
Dirk Sermeus

The model represents a vehicle of the 2nd Battalion, 3rd Panzer Regiment, 2nd Panzer Division during the Normandy invasion, in the vincinity of Caumont, where this division was used to stem the Allied advance. The model was built almost out of the box (I used the Dragon kit, late production with *Zimmerit*) but Friul tracks were added. The figures are Dragon but the heads came from Hornet. The painting, airbrushing and weathering was done with Tamiya and Vallejo acrylics and Humbrol enamels. The weathering is with MIG pigments, AV interactive and Tamiya pastels. The paint chipping was applied by brush and sponge technique.

Panzer IV
AUSF H
1:16 Scale
Brian Richardson

Trumpeter's 16th scale Panzer IV Ausf H out of the box is a very complex kit with 1816 parts on 81 sprues (one clear), 198 PE (7 frets), copper tow cable, metal barrel, 4 springs, 2 large decal sheets and a 52 page instruction book. Even with all this there's still room for improvement. I decided on trying for a Mid production Ausf H as the upper hull has the correct driver's hatch and turret ring splash guards so less surgery was required. The H model was also up armoured initially with 30mm plates bolted to the front 50mm vertical surfaces, later single 80mm plate was used along with thicker turret roof armour and this is depicted in the kit. Another important change made during production was the elimination of side vision ports to the superstructure and again the kit doesn't have these. Most early H's that had bolt-on armour seem to have vision ports but at least one photo in W Trojca's book shows an up armoured H without side vision blocks. Apparently field workshops often interchanged parts from the earlier Ausf. G and H making identification for us modellers at times difficult. Early on I wanted to finish this Panzer differently to the instructions which gives 4 camouflaged options; I settled on plain dark yellow as period photos of the 16th Panzer Division Ausf H's were finished this way. I've used some artistic license as I don't have an actual photo of this particular Ausf H – not every vehicle was photographed. My final step was to go over all high-wear areas, especially the tracks, with a 2B pencil for that bare steel look.

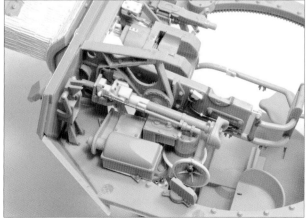

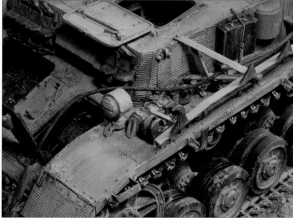

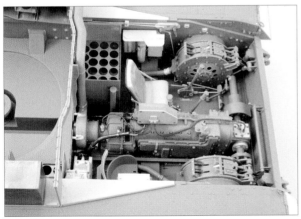

Panzer IV
AUSF.D/TAUCH
1:35 Scale
Bill Goodrich

The kit used is the Tristar kit #023, which is now being reissued by HobbyBoss (kit HB-80132). The model was built out of the box using no after-market products. The kit includes workable suspension and workable track. There is an interior for the turret, but nothing for the inside of the hull. The kit contains all the parts necessary to build a regular Ausf D, or a Tauch ready for submersion. I built an Ausf D/Tauch as would have been used in non-wading mode. It was painted with Tamiya German Gray (tank and tracks). Kit decals were used and it was weathered with oils and #2 pencil. The unditching beam is not included in the kit, though the brackets are. I used a section of bamboo skewer.

Panzer IV
AUSF F2 JUNE 1942 RUSSIA
1:35 Scale
Brian Bocchino

This is Dragon's smart kit for the Panzer IV Ausf F2. The entire hull has to be the best kit I have ever built. The turret construction wasn't bad either. I would rate this as one of my favorite builds to date.

Hobbyboss 1:35 German Sturmpanzer Iv Early Sd. Kfz.166 'Brummbar' – 80134

This Chinese kit from HobbyBoss is quality designed for the serious modeller. Although HobbyBoss are a relatively new company, they have spent a lot of time producing models for Trumpeter and appear to be very experienced in creating well-made injection-moulded kits. One such kit is the 1:35 Sturmpanzer IV early Sd.Kfz.166 which was built on the chassis of a PzKpfw. IV. The instructions are easy to read and follow, and the yellow mouldings are detailed and complete. The kit comprises of realistic photo etched parts that enhances the vehicle's additional features. Whilst you do not get metal tracks, these can be modified to be fully workable and look very real with sag. The HobbyBoss early Sturmpanzer IV is a worthy kit for any modeller wishing to build a late variant tank.

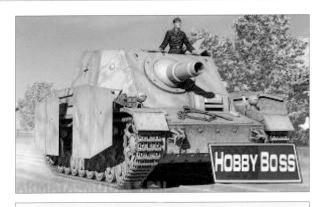

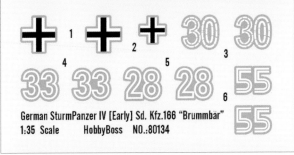

German SturmPanzer IV [Early] Sd. Kfz.166 "Brummbär"
1:35 Scale   HobbyBoss   NO.:80134

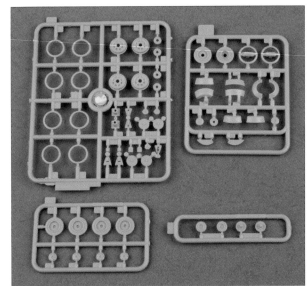

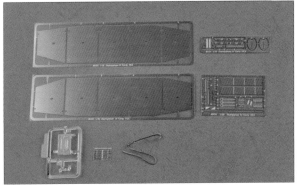

Trumpeter 1/35 3.7cm Flak 43 Flakpanzer IV Ostwind 01520 – TRM01520.

The Ostwind was based on the chassis of the late production Ausf J hull with the larger turret which allowed additional space for the crew. In kit form Trumpeter have produced a unique model of this flakpanzer that comes complete with 852 parts (628 for the vehicle and 224 individual track links) on 22 sprues and moulded in standard grey plastic. It also comes complete with a decal sheet and useful comprehensive instruction booklet. The model has comparatively accurate features including a well-produced Flak43 gun and realistic suspension and running gear. Detailing on the upper hull has been reproduced well and there are some good features. It includes separate vision port visors that look good, but it is important to note that these were not fitted to production Ostwinds. Other than that, a reasonably good model kit showing a late variant converted vehicle.

German 3.7cm Flak 43 Flakpanzer IV "Ostwind"
1/35 SCALE

Tamiya

Tamiya offers a variety of quality model kits for the Panzer IV modeller. One kit model that stands out among the Panzer IV model range is the 1/48 scale plastic model assembly kit of the late production Pzkpfw IV Ausf H. This kit has amazing track detail and out of the box the standard of the plastic mould kit is superb – very clean and crisp. Other quality Tamiya model kits for the Panzer IV include the 1/35 Pzkpfw IV Ausf D tank kit, the 1/35 Pzkpfw IV Ausf J tank model, the 1/35 Sturmgeschütz IV 1/35 kit and the 1/48 German Flakpanzer IV Wirbelwind with figures.

Hasegawa 1/72 Sd.Kfz.162 JagdPanzer IV L/48 'Early Version' – MT049 HSGMT049

Whilst Hasegawa have produced a new improved kit, one problem with this Jagdpanzer IV is the tracks, which are not that realistic. However, saying that, the rest of the model is superb, and I think any modeller with any degree of inventiveness will be able to adapt the tracks. The upper whole of the model has been well designed, and the interlocking armoured plates are impressive. There are a number of holes in the hull for the installation of various options included in the kit, which is a bonus. You can adapt the vehicle and select mono or binocular periscopes, and there are one or two machine-gun ports for the Jagdpanzer. The decals too are quite good and well printed. Though the markings are not extensive the painting guides are excellent. The only thing that lets the kit down is the lack of *Zimmerit* mine paste, which was applied to these vehicles as standard during the late war period. However, all it takes is a proficient modeller to enhance the kit with an application of *Zimmerit*, some foliage, and this will make quite a unique showcase model.

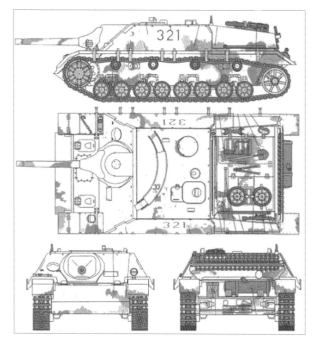

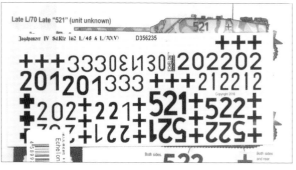

Armourfast 1/72 Pz Kpfw IV Ausf D (2 Kits in Box) ARM99028

Armourfast have introduced this basic model kit onto the market aimed at the beginner, the serious modeller and the war gamer that enjoys working with conversions. There are some 36 parts, two track units, upper hull, hull underside, the infamous 7.5cm cannon, gun mantle, turret front, two hatches, cupola, stowage bin, hull plate and turret pin and some rear hull details. Detailing on the upper and lower hull has been reproduced well and there are some good features. The kit will appeal to various modellers, and when you have completed putting the parts together, which are often easy to construct, the tank is comparatively a decent model.

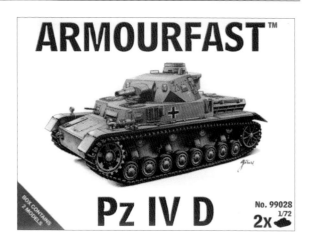

Revell Monogram 1/32 Panzer IV Tank Plastic Model Kit – 85-7861

Revell's late variant model Ausf H is a unique kit, that looks very realistic. This 197-piece model kit comes with two crew members and separate hatch covers, moulded in olive and black vinyl with optional side skirts and turret ring. There are also extra track links for additional armoured protection and other equipment. What makes this kit even more appealing is that there is a battle damaged option too, where there are holes in the side of the skirts to show where anti-tank shots have entered its armour. The modeller can also remove some of the side skirts for extra battle-shot realism. All in all Revell have produced a good model.

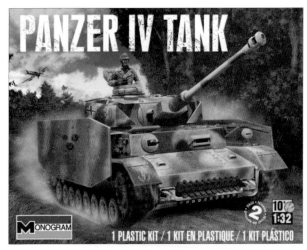

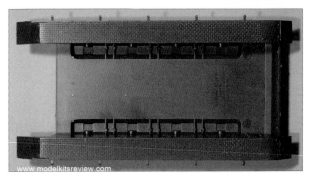

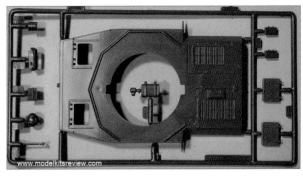

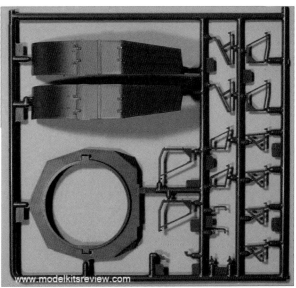

Dragon 1/35 Panzer IV Ausf F2 (G) – 6360

This is a relatively accurate kit and unlike previous models the muffler width, gun housing, hatch lock opening and a number of other details have been correctly produced by Dragon. The model comes complete in 505 parts in light grey plastic, there are 108 individual links, 15 clear plastic parts, 1 small etched fret with 26 parts, 1 length of braided steel wire, and a well-detailed decal and instruction sheet. All in all the model is very accurate and has better detail definition than most. The Ausf F2/G variant is a great model and the only negative is a few instruction issues with some parts incorrectly numbered and other parts not included. However, any keen modeller will overcome this comparatively small hurdle and build a very decent showcase.

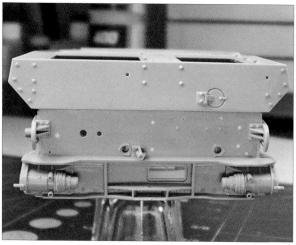

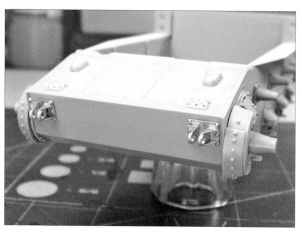

Vintage Mattel German WWII Tank Panzer IV, 1/32 Scale – 6859

This is a classic Monogram kit that has been well designed and is realistic. The instructions are clear, and the model easy to build. The kit is primarily aimed for a beginner to a mid-range modeller. Though basic and not as intricate as other models on the market, for the price it's worth the purchase. The kit is an accurate Pzkpfw IV, and with minimal painting, it certainly has the potential with a little ingenuity to make it a show piece. The kit will take roughly two to three hours to construct, and with a little paint, adding some weathering and battle-worn features, it's the perfect kit for a beginner.

Italeri No 6217 Pz.Kpfw.IV Ausf F1/F2 1/35

This kit is regarded among the modelling world as relatively decent. The lower hull tub is very good with its separate suspension details and the idler wheel mounts are exceptional. There are separate exhausts, but no smoke grenade discharging racks which was often found on this variant. On the hull front there are alternate crew hatches with signal ports, but the turret is quite basic and there is a noticeable lack of weld seams. However, this can be easily remedied by sanding, gluing and painting these areas. The commander's cupola comes in two parts and is moulded into the turret, which looks real. Also, what makes this kit good is that the modeller can choose which gun he requires. It comes with three different cannons starting with the early short barrelled 7.5cm KwK37 L/24 of the Ausf F1, and the longer 7.5cm KwK40 L/43 complete with muzzle brake (Ausf F2), and double baffle muzzle brake (Ausf G). The rest of the hull comes with moulded tools, the tracks are vinyl but you can get them to sag with a little persistence.

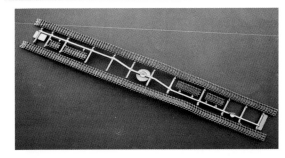

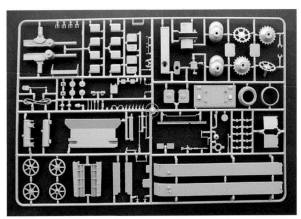

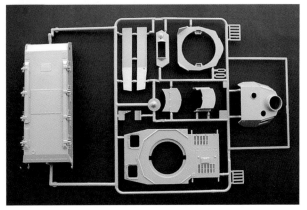

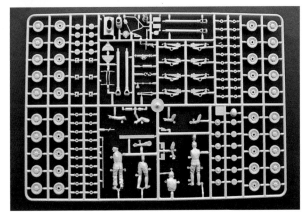

Airfix Panzer IV F1/F2 Tank 1:76 Scale – Product A0230

This Airfix kit will appeal to scale modellers, and when you have completed putting together its 101 small, fiddly pieces the tank is a relatively decent model. It does show signs of age as the detailing and parts are not completely up to modern standards which is probably why Airfix have stopped producing it (kits can still be found at various retailers). Nonetheless once painted its quite realistic. Adding extra camouflage such as foliage and making it travel and battle damaged creates better authenticity, especially as it was the primary tank used in the Second World War. Even the tracks look quite genuine with sag, and adding dirt and dust to them makes it quite a unique little model.

Panzerjäger and Flak Vehicles

In spite of the terrible setbacks on the Eastern Front the PzKpfw IV continued to prove its worth on the battlefield. In order to increase the strength of the Panzerwaffe in the East a variety of modified tanks using the chassis of the PzKpfw IV were seen in action during the last year of the war. The Sturmgeschütz IV for instance was one vehicle that had entered service in Russia on the chassis of a PzKpfw IV.

Another tank to make its debut during the latter period of the war was the Jagdpanzer IV which reached the Panzerjäger battalions of the Panzer divisions in small numbers until the end of the war. The Jagdpanzer IV was a very effective Panzer hunter and scored considerable successes during a number of actions. However, like many of the vehicles that entered service during the latter stages of the war, they were too few or too dispersed to do more than temporarily halt the advancing Russian army.

During the last year of the war, as further setbacks beset the Panzerwaffe, more modified vehicles came off the production line, many of which were on the chassis of a PzKpfw IV. One such vehicle was the Sturmpanzer (assault tank), which was basically a heavy 15cm infantry gun mounted on the chassis of a PzKpfw IV. However, it soon became obvious that the vehicle, with an ammunition load of 38 shells, a five-man crew and a fighting weight of 28.2 tons, was heavily overloaded.

Apart from the building of tanks to repel the huge quantities of enemy vehicles on the battlefield, it was also apparent that there was an urgent need to protect the infantry from enemy aircraft attack, which was causing massive losses to both men and equipment. Armoured vehicles were defenceless against these enemy aircraft, and for that reason a new Flakpanzer entered service. It was known as the 2cm Flakvierling 38 Flakpanzer IV, which was mounted on the chassis of a PzKpfw IV. The vehicle was literally a self-propelled mount for the quadruple 2cm Flakvierling 38 or 3.7cm Flak 43 anti-aircraft gun protected by a steel box bolted to the chassis floor. Although the crew had sufficient room on board especially when the sides were folded down, it was still very prone to enemy attack. Other variations of the vehicle were also produced in small numbers such as the 3.7cm Flak 43 Panzer IV Mobelwagen. In 1944 some 240 of these vehicles were built.

Other tanks which saw active service in small numbers were the Wirbelwind,

Ostwind and Kugelblitz, all of which were anti-aircraft tanks on the chassis of repaired or rebuilt PzKpfw IVs.

Aside from anti-aircraft tanks was the increased use of self-propelled mounts on either the chassis of the PzKpfw III or IV. Back in 1942 there had been a drastic requirement for motorized artillery to be deployed in action at a moment's notice. For this reason the Germans adopted the concept of self-propelled artillery mounts such as the heavy field 15cm howitzer mounted on a tank, known as the Hummel (Bumblebee) tank destroyer. The Hummel had an open-topped lightly armoured fighting compartment at the back of the vehicle which housed both the howitzer and the crew. The engine was moved to the centre of the vehicle to make room for this compartment. Late model Hummels had a slightly redesigned driver compartment and

Two photographs showing another variant built on the chassis of a PzKpfw IV Ausf H called the Sturmpanzer. These vehicles were known as the 'Brummbar' (literally, growling bear). It mounted a powerful 15cm sIG gun. Note the extensive application of *zimmerit*.

A new Flakpanzer IV Mobelwagen (SdKfz 161/3) just out of production. This vehicle was armed with the 3.7cm Flak 43 which was mounted on a PzKpfw IV Ausf J chassis. The first 20 units were completed by March 1944. A total of 240 of these mobile flak vehicles were produced by March 1945.

The Flakpanzerkampwagen IV (2cm Flakvierling 38) (SdKfz 161/4) self-propelled anti-aircraft gun, known as the Wirbelwind. These were assembled on rebuilt PzKpfw IV chassis that had been returned to Germany. This one is based on the Ausf G variant and identifiable by the 30mm armour plates welded to the front and superstructure.

Flakpanzer IV Mobelwagen undergoing maintenance. This vehicle was built on the chassis of a PzKpfw IV Ausf J. It is painted in dark yellow RAL 7028 with a camouflaged scheme of small red-brown RAL 8017 and large olive green RAL 6003 patches.

Two photographs showing the Flakpanzer IV Wirbelwind somewhere on the Western Front in 1944. These vehicles were built on the PzKpfw IV Ausf G chassis and have standard three-colour camouflage paint scheme of green and brown patches on the dark sand base.

A self-propelled artillery vehicle to see its debut in 1943 was the Hummel. The Hummel (Bumblebee) was gun adapted and mounted on the Geschützwagen III/IV chassis and armed with a 15cm howitzer. This Panzerfeldhaubitze 18M auf Geschützwagen III/IV (Sf) Hummel, SdKfz 165 entered service in 1943. Initially, designers had wanted to mount a 10.5cm leFH 18 howitzer on the chassis of a PzKpfw III, but it was rejected in favour of the more powerful and larger PzKpfw IV chassis.

front superstructure, to offer more room to the radio operator and driver.

Another variant to the Hummel, which mounted the self-propelled 8.8cm PaK 43/1, was the Nashorn (Rhinoceros). During the first half of 1943, this new model was introduced into production. The difference between this model and the Hummel was almost indistinguishable. Total production of the Nashorn amounted to some 494 vehicles, of which most were built in 1943. Since January 1944, the Germans, however, favoured the production of the newer tank destroyer, the Jagdpanzer IV, which had a much thicker armour plate if a less powerful 7.5cm gun. Production of the Nashorn continued until the end of the war but in low numbers.

Panzerjäger IV vehicles
Hornisse/Nashorn
8.8cm PaK on chassis of a PzKpfw III/IV
Sturmgeschütz IV
Elefant, last Panzerjäger vehicle designated

Later generation Jagdpanzer
7.5cm PaK 39 L/48 gun/modified version
7.5cm StuK 40 L/48 mounted on the chassis of a Sturmgeschütz III/IV assault gun

Jagdpanzer IV
7.5cm 42 L/70 gun on the chassis of a PzKpfw IV

Self-propelled artillery (providing close fire-support for infantry and acting as specialized tank destroying vehicles)
Hummel
15cm howitzer on chassis of a PzKpfw III/IV

1. Vertical columns of horizontal ridges
- PzKpfw III
- PzKpfw IV Ausf H, J
- PzBefWg IV
- Sturmgeschütz III
- Sturmgeschütz IV
- Panzerjäger IV
- Panzer IV/70
- Sturmpanzer
- Wirbelwind
- Ostwind
- PzKpfw V Panther
- Pz Kpfw VI Tiger
- Panzersturmmörser
- Jagdtiger

2. Horizontal columns of vertical ridges
- Sturmgeschütz Ausf G
- PzKpfw IV Ausf H
- PzKpfw V Panther Ausf G

3. Horizontal columns of vertical ridges with one-way diagonal groves
- PzKpfw V Panther Ausf G

4. Horizontal columns of vertical ridges with vertical groves, separating the columns into small boxes
- Sturmgeschütz
- P.Kpfw V Panther Ausf A, G

Top right A Hummel on the move during operations in the summer of 1943. This vehicle is painted in a base colour of RAL 7028 and has a camouflage scheme of thin red-brown lines of RAL 8017 and olive green 6003.

Above: Two Hummels on a road in 1944. The fighting compartment, though large for tank hunting standards, was often cramped as the gun's recoil and the discarding of empty shells meant there was little room.

Photograph of the Geschützwagen III/IV sFH18/1 (SF), more commonly known as the Hummel. This heavy self-propelled gun carried 18 15cm rounds and was a potent weapon against Soviet armour.

The crew of a Panzerfeldhaubitze 18M auf Geschützwagen III/IV (Sf) Hummel, SdKfz 165 sitting on their vehicle during a pause in their drive through a destroyed town in 1943. A total of 714 of these vehicles were built, but by early February 1944 Hitler suspended production as he thought these were no longer suitable as fighting machines.

A Hummel parked at a training barracks in 1943.

Alongside the Hummel was another self-propelled vehicle that made its debut at Kursk. This was known as the Nashorn (Rhinoceros) – initially nicknamed in mid-1943 Hornisse (Hornet). It looked similar to the Hummel, but was a light turretless vehicle that mounted a PaK 43 heavy anti-tank gun. The Nashorn entered production in early 1943; during this period of transformation it was given numerous official designations: 8.8cm PaK 43 (L/71) auf Fahrgestell Panzerkampfwagen III/IV (Sf) or 8.8cm PaK 43 (L/71) auf Geschützwagen III/IV (SdKfz 164), and as a Panzerjäger Hornisse.

A battery of whitewashed Nashorns during an enemy action in the winter of 1944. The Nashorn fought with considerable success on all fronts; there were six heavy Panzerjäger *abteilungen* (battalions) each equipped with 30 Nashorns: the 88th, 93rd, 519th, 525th, 560th and 655th. The 525th Panzerjäger Abteilung served in Italy during 1944.

The Sturmgeschütz IV (StuG IV) (SdKfz 167) pictured here with crew, was based on the PzKpfw IV chassis used during the latter part of war. It mounts the StuK 40 in a cast *topfblende* (pot mantle). From December 1943 to May 1945, Krupp built 1,108 StuG IVs and converted an additional 31 from battle-damaged PzKpfw IVs brought back to Germany for conversion.

A side view of the Panzerfeldhaubitze 18M auf Geschützwagen III/IV (Sf) Hummel, SdKfz 165 undergoing maintenance at a workshop in Poland in the summer of 1944. A crewmember can be seen in the driver's compartment

A rare photograph of what appears to be a pre-production version of the Jagdpanzer IV, designated as the Jagdpanzer IV A-O. It has a curved superstructure front and is armed with two MG ports as well as a muzzle brake on the 7.5cm PaK 39 L/48 cannon.

The crew on a Hummel on a flatbed railway car. When the Hummel came off the production line in the first half of 1943 it was tested and put through its paces, and then signed off. It made its debut at Kursk in June/July 1943 when some 100 Hummels were in service. These vehicles served in armoured artillery battalions or Panzerartillerie *Abteilungen* of the Panzer divisions, forming separate heavy self-propelled artillery batteries, each with six Hummels and one ammunition carrier.

5. Small squares
• Sturmgeschütz
• PzKpfw V Panther Ausf A, G
• Jagdpanther

6. Square waffle-type patterns
• Sturmgeschütz Ausf G
• Sturmhaubitze
• PzKpfw V Panther
• PzKpfw VI Tiger Ausf E

7. Horizontal columns of vertical ridges with the ridges being diagonal, and changing direction for every column
• PzKpfw IV

8. Horizontal columns of vertical ridges with diagonal groves going both ways forming rhomb-like figures
• PzKpfw V Panther

9. Vertical columns of horizontal ridges, separating the columns into small boxes
• Sturmgeschütz
• PzKpfw V Panther Ausf G

10. Waffle-type pattern with rhombs
• Sturmgeschütz

11. Continuous vertical ridges
• PzKpfw V Panther
• SdKfz 251 Ausf D

German armoured vehicle colour glossary

September 1939
All German armoured vehicles were painted in a two-tone scheme of dark grey and dark brown. Dark grey numbered RAL 7021 was the base coat. Irregularly shaped patches of dark brown numbered RAL 7017 were to be spray-painted onto one-third of the surface.

June 1940
A general order was issued to stop applying patches of dark brown and only use dark grey for the entire surface.

February 1943
A general order was issued to change the base coat from dark grey to dark yellow numbered RAL 7028 – a tan colour. Field units were issued with tins of red-brown RAL 8017 and dark olive green RAL 6003 paste concentrate to create camouflage patterns suitable for local conditions. This practice continued after Panzers were covered with anti-magnetic *zimmerit* starting in August 1943.

August 1944
An order was issued to the assembly firms to apply the camouflage pattern at the assembly plant using dark yellow RAL 7028 as the base coat with olive green RAL 6003 and red-brown RAL 8017 applied in patches. This order created the uniform pattern, which has become known as the 'ambush' camouflage scheme. Following the order to stop the use of *zimmerit* in September 1944, Panzers left the assembly plants with a base coat of primer of dark red RAL 8012 with only about half of the surface covered with patches of red-brown, olive green, or dark yellow.

November 1944
The Panzers were to receive a base coat of dark green RAL 6003. A camouflage pattern was to be created at the assembly plant by

spraying on red-brown or dark yellow in sharp contours. Camouflage paint colours were authorized for use in hot climates or in the winter.

Primary German Armoured Vehicle Colours 1939–45

1. Afrika Brown RAL 8020
2. Blue Grey (RAL 7016)
3. Brown (RAL 8017
4. Dark Yellow (RAL 7028)
5. Dark Grey (7021)
6. Ivory (1001)
7. Field Grey (RAL 6006)
8. Yellow Brown (RAL 8000)
9. Yellow (RAL 1006)
10. Grey (RAL 7027)
11. Grey Green (RAL 7008)
12. Green (RAL 6007)
13. Olive Green (6003)
14. Red (RAL 3000)
15. Red-brown (RAL 8012)
16. Black (RAL 9005)
17. Signal Brown (RAL 8002)
18. White 1 (RAL 9001)
19. White 2 (RAL 9002)

Panzer Division Glossary

1st Panzer Division
Formed: October 1935 at Weimer
Divisional insignia: The division chose a white oak leaf emblem, and this was first used in the Polish campaign in September 1939. In France in 1940, the oak leaf was extensively used. For preparation against Russia a new symbol was designed, a yellow inverted Y. However, the painting of the new divisional sign was not widely liked by the crews and the emblem was applied on leading vehicles, whilst the older style oak leaf was retained on support vehicles. From 1943–45, the use of the white oak leaf was still seen many vehicles and was unofficially accepted by OKW.

Units:
Panzer Regiment 1
Panzer Artillery Regiment 73
Panzergrenadier Regiments 1, 113
Panzer Reconnaissance Battalion 1

Theatres of operation:
Poland 1939
Belgium and France 1940
Eastern Front Northern and Central Groups June 1941–February 1943
Balkans and Greece 1943
Ukraine November–December 1943
Hungary and Austria June 1944–May 1945

2nd Panzer Division
Formed: October 1935 at Wurzburg
Divisional insignia: The divisional insignia first made its appearance during the Polish campaign. Its emblem was a pair of solid yellow circles. This same symbol was used in France the following year. For the invasion of Russia the division used a new inverted Y with one mark. This was used during the first two years of the campaign in Russia. During mid-1943 a white trident sign replaced this emblem. The trident was used for the remainder of the war.

Units:
Panzergrenadier Regiments 2, 304
Panzer Regiment 3
Panzer Artillery Regiment 74
Panzer Reconnaissance Battalion 2

Theatres of operation:
Poland 1939
France 1940
Balkans and Greece 1941
Army Group Centre (Smolensk, Orel, Kiev) 1942–43
France and Germany 1944–45

3rd Panzer Division
Formed: October 1935 at Berlin
Divisional insignia: The divisional sign was a yellow E lying on its side, face down. It was first seen in Poland in 1939. Seven months later in May 1940 the same emblem was used in the Low Countries and France. For the invasion of Russia a new sign was introduced and was regarded as the official sign. It was an inverted yellow Y with two marks. In spite of the new sign, units of the division could use the bear in a white shield, and the tanks in the 6th Panzer Regiment also used the standing bear without a shield. The bear was often painted in various colours that included, white, yellow, blue and red. In 1943 the 6th Panzer Regiment adopted a regimental emblem that comprised of a black shield that was round on the bottom and flat on top, with the 1939–40 divisional sign of the 4th Panzer Regiment, and a pair of crossed swords below this.

Units:
Panzergrenadier Regiments 3, 394
Panzer Regiment 6
Panzer Artillery Regiment 75
Panzer Reconnaissance Battalion 3

Theatres of operation:
Poland 1939
France 1940
Central Russia 1941–42
Southern Russia (Kharkov, Dnepr Bend) 1943
Ukraine and Poland 1944
Hungary and Austria 1944–45

4th Panzer Division
Formed: November 1938 at Wurzburg
Divisional insignia: This divisional sign was identified as a three-pointed star and was first seen during its advance through Poland. The following year during its armoured spearhead through France it displayed a man-rune enclosed within a circle. In 1941 for the Russian campaign the division used the inverted Y with three marks, and used this for the remainder of the war.

Units:
Panzergrenadier Regiments 12, 33
Panzer Regiment 35
Panzer Artillery Regiment 103
Panzer Reconnaissance Battalion 4

Theatres of operation:
Poland 1939
France 1940
Eastern Front 1942–44
Caucasus 1942
Kursk 1943
Latvia 1944
Germany 1945

5th Panzer Division
Formed: November 1939 at Oppeln
Divisional insignia: No divisional signs were used in Poland, but in France the symbol was identified as an inverted Y with one round dot. In late September 1940 the division lost the 15th Panzer Regiment to the 11th Panzer Division. The division saw service in the Balkans, using the new symbol of one yellow X. The 5th Panzer Division then saw service on the Eastern Front. The 31st Panzer Regiment adopted the red devil's head as a regimental symbol. This emblem, together with the yellow X, was used until the end of the war.

Units:
Panzergrenadier Regiments 13, 14
Panzer Regiment 31
Panzer Artillery Regiment 116
Panzer Reconnaissance Battalion 5

Theatres of operation:
France 1941
Yugoslavia and Greece 1941
Eastern Front (Kursk, Dnepr, Latvia, Kurland) 1941–44
East Prussia 1944–45

6th Panzer Division
Formed: October 1939 at Wuppertal
Divisional insignia: The appearance of the division's emblem consisting of a yellow inverted Y with two round dots was seen in France, 1940. For the Russian campaign it used the letter symbol X in yellow. During the drive on Moscow a yellow 'war hatchet' was used as a temporary sign.

Units:
Panzergrenadier Regiments 4, 114
Panzer Regiment 11
Panzer Artillery Regiment 76
Panzer Reconnaissance Battalion 6

Theatres of operation:
France 1944
Eastern Front 1941–44
Hungary and Austria 1944–45

7th Panzer Division
Formed: October 1939 at Weimar
Divisional insignia: The division's emblem was first seen in France and was a yellow inverted Y with three dots. For Operation Barbarossa the division adopted a new sign, a yellow Y. The division fought mercilessly in Russia and retained the yellow Y until the end of the war.

Units:
Panzergrenadier Regiments 6, 7
Panzer Regiment 25
Panzer Artillery Regiment 78
Panzer Reconnaissance Battalion 7

Theatres of operation:
France 1940
Central Russia 1941
France 1942 (refit)
Southern Russia (Kharkov) 1942
Baltic Coast and Prussia 1944 45

8th Panzer Division
Formed: October 1938 at Berlin
Divisional insignia: This division's sign made its debut in France in 1940, using a yellow Y with one round dot. In Russia the division used a new sign, a yellow Y with one yellow mark. It was used until the end of the war.

Units:
Panzergrenadier Regiments 8, 28
Panzer Regiment 10

Panzer Artillery Regiment 80
Panzer Reconnaissance Battalion 8

Theatres of operation:
Holland and France 1940
Balkans 1941
Southern Russia 1941
Central Russia 1942
Kursk 1943
France 1944
Ardennes 1944–45

10th Panzer Division
Formed: April 1939 at Stuttgart
Divisional insignia: This divisional sign was first seen during the French campaign in 1940 and carried the official sign of a yellow Y with three round dots. The 7th Panzer Regiment adopted the silhouette of a bison, and this marking was commonly found on tanks in this division. For the invasion of Russia the emblem was officially a yellow Y with three marks. It retained the sign until it was finally destroyed in Tunisia in 1943.

Units:
Panzergrenadier Regiments 69, 86
Panzer Regiment 7
Panzer Artillery Regiment 90
Panzer Reconnaissance Battalion 10

Theatres of operation:
Poland 1939
France 1940
France 1942
Tunisia 1943 (division destroyed)

11th Panzer Division
Formed: August 1940 at Breslau
Divisional insignia: This division received the official sign of a yellow circle divided by a vertical bar and was formed in late 1940. The division's personal emblem was a white-stencilled figure of a ghost brandishing a sword. Because of this emblem the division became known as the 'Ghost' division, and fought until the end of the war.

Units:
Panzergrenadier Regiments 110, 111
Panzer Regiment 15
Panzer Artillery Regiment 119
Panzer Reconnaissance Battalion 11

Theatres of operation:
Balkans 1941
Eastern Front (Orel, Belgorod, Krivoi Rog, Korsun) 1941–44
Northern France 1944

12th Panzer Division
Formed: October 1940
Divisional insignia: Although formed in late 1940, this divisional insignia what not seen extensively until it saw action on the Eastern Front. Its symbol was a yellow circle divided into three equal segments by a Y. The division did not modify its insignia and it carried it through the rest of the war.

Units:
Panzergrenadier Regiments 5, 25
Panzer Regiment 29
Panzer Artillery Regiment 2
Panzer Reconnaissance Battalion 12

Theatres of operation:
Eastern Front Army Group Centre 1941–44
Eastern Front (Minsk, Smolensk) 1941
Leningrad 1942
Orel and Middle Dnepr 1943
Kurland 1945 (captured by the Red Army)

13th Panzer Division
Formed: October 1940
Divisional insignia: This division primarily served on the Eastern Front and also in Hungary. It retained its emblem of a yellow circle divided into squares until the end of the war.

Units:
Panzergrenadier Regiments 66, 93
Panzer Regiment 4
Panzer Artillery Regiment 13
Panzer Reconnaissance Battalion 13

Theatre of operations:
Rumania 1941
Eastern Front 1941–44
Kiev 1942
Caucasus and the Kuban 1943–44
Krivoi Rog 1944
Germany 1944
Hungary 1944–45

14th Panzer Division
Formed: August 1940
Divisional insignia: The division's sign first made its debut in the Balkans in 1941. The division saw action in Russia where it was consequently destroyed at Stalingrad in 1942. However, a new 14th Panzer Division was formed in France following the catastrophe at Stalingrad, and returned to the Eastern Front in 1943. The divisional sign was a diamond with the lower sides extended to form an X.

Units:
Panzergrenadier Regiments 103,108
Panzer Regiment 36
Panzer Artillery Regiment 4
Panzer Reconnaissance Battalion 14

Theatres of operation:
Yugoslavia 1941
Germany 1941
Hungary 1941
Yugoslavia 1941
Southern Russia 1941
Caucasus December 1942 (annihilated at Stalingrad)
France 1943 (division re-formed)
Southern Russia 1943–44
Germany 1945

15th Panzer Division
Formed: August 1940
Divisional insignia: This division's insignia made its appearance in North Africa in April 1941. The signs were a triangle divided by a vertical bar, mainly seen painted in black, red or white. The 8th Panzer Regiment had a regimental symbol of a wolf-trap that was normally painted in red. As part of the Deutsches Afrika Korps, or DAK, all the vehicles in this division carried the white palm tree insignia of this korps.

Units:
Panzergrenadier Regiments 104,115
Panzer Regiment 8
Panzer Artillery Regiment 33
Panzer Reconnaissance Battalion 15

Theatres of operation:
North Africa 1941–43 (surrendered in Tunisia 1943)

16th Panzer Division
Formed: August 1940
Divisional insignia: This divisional insignia received a Y with one bar across the shaft. Its emblem was seen on the Eastern Front until it was destroyed at Stalingrad in late 1942. A new division was formed in France in 1943 and received the same symbol. Sometimes though the sign was outlined in black. The reason for the black marking is not really known, but it probably suggests that the division was

paying its respects to the loss of the first formation.

Units:
Panzergrenadier Regiments 64, 79
Panzer Regiment 2
Panzer Artillery Regiment 16
Panzer Reconnaissance Battalion 16

Theatres of Operation:
Southern Russia 1941
Caucasus December 1942 (annihilated at Stalingrad)
France 1943 (division re-formed)
Italy 1943
Russia (Kiev) 1943–44
Czechoslovakia 1945 (surrendered)

17th Panzer Division
Formed: October 1940
Divisional insignia: This division's emblem was entirely seen on the Eastern Front and was applied with a yellow Y with two bars across the shaft.

Units:
Panzergrenadier Regiments 40, 63
Panzer Regiment 39
Panzer Artillery Regiment 27
Panzer Reconnaissance Battalion 17

Theatres of operation:
Eastern Front Central and Southern Sectors 1941–45

18th Panzer Division
Formed: October 1940
Divisional insignia: The division's emblem was a yellow Y with three bars across its shaft. The 8th Panzer Brigade had a special marking, but this was not a divisional emblem. It had a shield edged white, with a white skull and lines of water in white. The division was disbanded in 1943 and reorganized as an artillery division, but continued using the same divisional sign.

Units:
Panzergrenadier Regiments 52,101
Panzer Regiment 18
Panzer Artillery Regiment 88
Panzer Reconnaissance Battalion 18

Theatres of operation:
Eastern Front Central and Southern Sectors 1941–43

19th Panzer Division
Formed: October 1940
Divisional insignia: Because of the area where the division was formed it adopted a yellow wolf-trap insignia. This emblem was seen on Panzers primarily on the Eastern Front, but the division did serve in Poland, notably in the Warsaw uprising in August 1944.

Units:
Panzergrenadier Regiments 73, 74
Panzer Regiment 27
Panzer Artillery Regiment 19
Panzer Reconnaissance Battalion 19

Theatres of operation:
Eastern Front Central and Southern Sectors 1941–44

20th Panzer Division
Formed: October 1940
Divisional insignia: The insignia of this division first appeared in October 1940 and was seen widely on the Eastern Front. Its symbol was a yellow E on its side, arms down, identical to the early 3rd Panzer Division emblem. In late 1943 the division received a new divisional insignia, which was a yellow arrow breaking through a curved borderline.

Units:
Panzergrenadier Regiments 59, 112
Panzer Regiment 21
Panzer Artillery Regiment 92
Panzer Reconnaissance Battalion 20

Theatres of operations:
Eastern Front 1941–44 (Moscow 1941, Orel 1943)
Rumania 1944
East Prussia 1944
Hungary 1944

21st Panzer Division
Formed: February 1941 in the field
Divisional insignia: This division carried the DAK palm tree sign as
well as the white D split by a horizontal line. This emblem did vary
and looked like a rectangle rather than a letter D. In northern France
in 1944 the new formation also used the D split by the bar, which
was painted either in white or yellow.

Units:
Panzergrenadier Regiments 125, 192
Panzer Regiment 22
Panzer Artillery Regiment 155
Panzer Reconnaissance Battalion 21

Theatres of operations:
North Africa 1941–43 (surrendered)
France 1943 (division re-formed)
Northern France 1944
Eastern Front 1945

22nd Panzer Division
Formed: October 1941 in France
Divisional insignia: The symbol of this division was a yellow arrow
with two bars across the shaft. The sign made its debut on the
Eastern Front in 1941. After it was almost annihilated at Stalingrad
the component units were distributed between the 7th and 23rd
Panzer divisions.

Units:
Panzergrenadier Regiments 129,140
Panzer Regiment 204
Panzer Artillery Regiment 140
Panzer Reconnaissance Battalion 140

Theatres of operations:
Russia Central Front 1942 (almost annihilated at Stalingrad)
Kharkov 1943 (dissolved)

23rd Panzer Division
Formed: October 1941 in France
Divisional insignia: The division adopted a personal emblem of a
white silhouette of the Eiffel Tower. Often, these two signs were
used together and they were seen in Russia, Poland, Hungary and
during the final weeks of the war.

Units:
Panzergrenadier Regiments 126, 128
Panzer Regiment 23
Panzer Artillery Regiment 128
Panzer Reconnaissance Battalion 23

Theatres of operation:
Eastern Front 1942–44
Kharkov 1943
Caucasus 1943
Dnepr Bend 1944)
Poland 1944 (refit)
Hungary 1944

24th Panzer Division
Formed: February 1942
Divisional insignia: Because this division was formed from the old

1st Cavalry Division the armoured force decided to retain its old
division's history with a 'Leaping horse and rider' sign. In late 1942
the division was destroyed at Stalingrad, but was re-formed in
France in 1943. The new division, however, replaced the 'Leaping
horse and rider' emblem with a simple bar leaping a barrier in the
open circle, often painted in yellow.

Units:
Panzergrenadier Regiments 21, 26
Panzer Regiment 24
Panzer Artillery Regiment 89
Panzer Reconnaissance Battalion 24

Theatres of operation:
Eastern Front 1942
Stalingrad 1942 (annihilated)
Northern France 1943 (re-formed)
Italy 1943
Eastern Front 1943
Kiev and Dnepr bend 1943
Poland 1944
Hungary 1944
Slovakia 1944
Germany 1945

25th Panzer Division
Formed: February 1942 from units in Norway
Divisional insignia: Activated in 1943 in Russia, this division had two
signs, but there is no photographic evidence of the more complex
second emblem. The most common of this divisions sign was a
stencil showing a row of three stars over a horizontal line over a
modified crescent. This was normally seen applied in either yellow
or white, though other colours like black were even used.

Units:
Panzergrenadier Regiments 146, 147
Panzer Regiment 9
Panzer Artillery Regiment 91
Panzer Reconnaissance Battalion 25

Theatres of operation:
Eastern Front Southern Sector 1943
Kiev 1943
Denmark 1944 (refit)
Poland 1944
Germany 1945

26th Panzer Division
Formed: October 1942 in Brittany
Divisional insignia: This divisional sign was painted in a complex
stencil of a Prussian grenadier's head in a circle and normally
painted in white. The sign was seen in Italy in 1943 and 1944, and
was the last Panzer division in Italy.

Units:
Panzergrenadier Regiments 9, 67
Panzer Regiment 26
Panzer Artillery Regiment 93
Panzer Reconnaissance Battalion 26

Theatres of operation:
Italy 1943–44

27th Panzer Division
Formed: 1942 in France
Divisional insignia: This divisional sign was a painted yellow arrow
with three bars across the shaft, and was very similar to that of
the 22nd Panzer Division. The division saw limited action and was
disbanded following heavy casualties in early 1943 at Stalingrad.

Theatres of operation:
Eastern Front 1942
Stalingrad 1942 (disbanded)

116th Panzer Division
Formed: 1944 in France
Divisional insignia: The sign for this division was a modification of that from the 16th Panzergrenadier Division of a greyhound running over ground, in white. The 116th Panzer, however, enclosed this greyhound emblem in a white oval.

Units:
Panzergrenadier Regiments 60, 156
Panzer Regiment 16
Panzer Artillery Regiment 146
Panzer Reconnaissance Battalion 116

Theatres of operations:
France 1944
Ardennes 1944
Kleve 1945

Panzer Lehr Division
Formed: 1944 in France
Divisional insignia: This crack armoured division was activated in the winter of 1943, and its symbol was the white script L. The division had three battalions, one of Panthers (1st Battalion) and the other of Panzerwagen IVs (3rd Battalion). The Panthers were not originally from Panzer Lehr but replacements from the 3rd Panzer Division. These Panthers used a larger white outline version of the Panzer Lehr script L. A number of Panzers too carried variations and company numbers in white next to small rhomboid outlines on the front and rear of the hulls.

Units:
Panzergrenadier Regiments 901, 902
Panzer Regiment 103
Panzer Artillery Regiment 130
Panzer Reconnaissance Battalion 130

Theatres of operation:
France 1944
Ardennes 1944
Holland 1944
Germany 1944

Panzer IV (PzKpfw IV) Variants

Production
Ausf A: 35 built (Krupp-Gruson) November 1937 & June 1938
Ausf B: 42 built (Krupp-Gruson) May–October 1938
Ausf C: 140 built (Krupp-Gruson) October 1938–August 1939.
Ausf D: 200 & 48 built (Krupp-Gruson) October 1939–October 1940
Ausf E: 206 built (Krupp-Gruson) October 1940–April 1941
Ausf F: 471 built (Krupp-Gruson, Vomag and Nibelungenwerke) April 1941–March 1942
Ausf F2: Designation for Ausf F chassis and later renamed
Ausf G: 1,927 built (Krupp-Gruson, Vomag and Nibelungenwerke) March 1942–June 1943
Ausf H: 2,324 built (Krupp-Gruson, Vomag and Nibelungenwerke) June 1943–February 1944
Ausf J: 3,160 built (Vomag Nibelungenwerke) February 1944–April 1945

Ausf A to Ausf F1
Ausf A
The Ausf A variant was the first and 35 of these versions left the production line. It was powered by a Maybach HL 108TR engine, SGR 75 transmission with five forward gears and one reverse and had a road speed of 19.26 mph. The tank's main armament was a Kampfwagenkanone 37 L/24 (KwK 37 L/24) 7.5cm (2.95 in) gun, which was a low-velocity gun primarily built to mainly fire high-explosive shells. Mounted coaxially with the main gun for

local defence was a 7.92 mm (0.31 in) MG 34 machine gun with the main gun in the turret, while a second machine gun of the same type was mounted in the front plate of the hull. The Ausf A variant was well protected by 14.5mm of steel armour bolted to the front plate of the chassis, and 20mm on the turret.

Ausf B
This was an improved 1937 version including a new engine powered by a Maybach HL 120TR, and an SSG 75 transmission, with six forward gears and one reverse gear and with an improved speed of 24 mph. The glacis plate was augmented to a maximum thickness of 30mm, and the hull-mounted machine gun was replaced by a covered pistol port. Forty-two of these variants left the factory before the next series was introduced.

An Ausf A on the front, which is quite a rare sight as only 35 of these models were produced. This one displays a white-outline Balkenkreuz on the superstructure and also had an underlined tactical number which is obstructed by the open hatch on the turret sides. This vehicle is distinguished as an Ausf A by the shape of the commander's cupola as well as the triangular frame-like device on the side of the superstructure, behind the national insignia.

A PzKpfw IV Ausf B during operations in the Polish campaign in September 1939. Note the white cross painted in white right of the tactical number 433. The white cross was painted in order to distinguish friend from foe on the battlefield, especially at a distance.

An Ausf B during operations in 1941 halted in a field. On this particular variant the glacis plate had been augmented to a maximum thickness of 30mm (1.18 in), a new driver's visor had been installed on the straightened hull front plate, and the hull-mounted MG34 machine gun has been replaced by a covered pistol port and visor flap. The superstructure width and ammunition stowage too have been reduced to save weight.

Ausf C

Built in 1938, it included minor modifications such as the turret armour increased to 30mm. After producing 40 of these models, a new HL 120TRM was installed. Production of these variants ceased in August 1939 with some 140 of them entering service.

Ausf D

This was a newly improved version of the Ausf C which included the hull machine gun being changed and the turret's internal gun mantlet altered to an external one. With armour upgraded, its side plates were increased to 20mm. 248 were manufactured. At end of September it was decided to scale up production of the PzKpfw IV, which was adopted for general use as the Sonderkraftfahrzeug 161 (SdKfz 161).

Ausf F2 to Ausf J

Ausf F2

In May/June 1941 it was decided to improve the PzKpfw IV main armament. This included integrating the same 5cm PaK 38 L/60 gun into the turret. The first prototype was to be delivered by 15 November 1941. Designers then decided to up-gun the vehicle by replacing the 5cm gun with a 7.5cm anti-tank gun, later known as 7.5cm PaK 40 L/46. Because the recoil length was too long for the tank's turret, the recoil mechanism and chamber were shortened. This resulted in the 7.5cm KwK 40 L/43. Initially, the gun was mounted with a single-chamber, ball-shaped muzzle brake, which provided just under half of the recoil system's braking ability. By 1942 the new upgraded longer-barrelled PzKpfw IV was known as the Ausf F2 with the designation SdKfz 161/1, and specifically manufactured to counter the Soviet T-34 and KV tanks. Some 175 of these Ausf F2 tanks were produced between March and

An Ausf B or C drives through a French town during operations on the Western Front in 1940. The vehicle is armed with the 7.5cm KwK L/24 gun. One of the distinguishing features between an Ausf B and a C was the visor and pistol port located in front of the radio operator's position. Another was the steep slope on the engine ventilation grilles which had three horizontal dividers instead of one as seen on later variants like the Ausf D.

An Ausf C leaves a training depot. This vehicle has a non-standard turret bustle stowage bin, which has probably been improvised. The tactical number 621 is painted in white and is on the centre of the bin and on the forward part of the turret.

Below left: This Ausf D belonging to the 10th Panzer Division trains its 7.5cm gun towards a possible target. Note the divisional insignia of a bison painted on the side of the turret. Initially, the divisional sign carried a yellow Y with three round dots. However, the 7th Panzer Regiment adopted the silhouette of a bison, commonly found on tanks in this division, during the French campaign.

An Ausf E converted to a Tauchpanzer from the 8th Company, 35th Panzer Regiment of the 4th Panzer Division. Behind it is a PzKpfw III Ausf G along with a PzKpfw II and another PzKpfw III converted to a Tauchpanzer. Additional armoured plates were fitted to the majority of PzKpfw IV Ausf Es and can be seen on the front and sides of the superstructure and sides of the lower hull.

An Ausf D advancing along a Russian road in the summer of 1941. The overall dark grey RAL 7021 factory finish is heavily powdered with pale dust. The Balkenkreuz has been stencil-painted on the superstructure side without first removing the radio antenna trough. The only visible marking is the three-digit tactical number on the rear of the turret box painted in white.

An Ausf E Vorpanzer. This vehicle was produced between September and April 1941. Modified from the Ausf D variant, the armour increased by 50mm on the bow plate and 20mm–30mm on the upper glacis; there was a new protective visor for the driver. Hatches were redesigned, and the turret rear now incorporated the commander's new cupola; potential weak areas in the hull rear were eliminated. Later, additional appliqué armour protection was added to the lower hull sides and suspension units to protect against anti-tank guns and mines.

An Ausf F parked near a building, probably a training depot. The new drive sprocket and idler design can be seen along with the two-piece turret side hatches. Other modifications include the turret traverse motor muffler, armoured smoke candle rack and a shorter muffler.

Two Ausf Fs painted in winter whitewash halted along a road in a village somewhere on the Eastern Front. Panzer crews typically utilized surrounding buildings as additional cover against ground or aerial attack.

July 1942. Three months after beginning production, the PzKpfw IV Ausf F2 was renamed Ausf G. There was hardly any difference between the F2 and early Ausf G models.

Ausf G

The production run for the Ausf G was between May 1942 and June 1943. Modifications included armoured plate increased to 80mm thick for frontal plates. Vision ports on either side of the turret were installed, and removed on the right turret front, while a rack for two spare road wheels was installed on the track guard on the left side of the hull. Complementing this, brackets for seven spare track links were added to the glacis plate. The engine's ventilation was improved by creating slits over the engine deck to the rear of the chassis, and cold weather performance was boosted by adding a device to heat the engine's coolant, as well as a starter fluid injector. On 19 March 1943, the first PzKpfw IV with side skirts or *schürzen* on its sides and turret entered service. The double hatch for the commander's cupola was replaced by a single round hatch from a very late model Ausf G. and the cupola was up-armoured as well. In April 1943, the KwK 40 L/43 was replaced by the longer 7.5cm KwK 40 L/48 gun, with a redesigned multi-baffle muzzle brake with improved recoil efficiency.

Ausf H

This variant was produced in April 1943 and received the designation SdKfz 161/2. Various modifications saw glacis armour improved by manufacturing it as a single 80mm plate. *Zimmerit* was added to all the vertical services of the tank armour. Its sides and turret were further protected by the addition of 5mm side skirts and 8mm turret skirts. Rubber return rollers with cast steel were added, and the hull also was fitted with triangular supports for the easily damaged side skirts.

Ausf J

This final variant went into production in 1944. Modifications comprised the removal of the electric generator that powered the tank's turret traverse. Instead the crew had to rotate the turret manually. The space was later used for the installation of an auxiliary 200-litre fuel tank, which increased the range of the vehicle to nearly 200 miles. The pistol and vision ports in the turret were removed, and the engine's radiator housing was simplified by changing the slanted sides to straight sides. Due to the lack of steel the PzKpfw IV side skirts were replaced by wire mesh, while to further speed up production the number of return rollers was reduced from four to three.

An Ausf G rolling along a road in the summer of 1942. This vehicle is still fitted with the turret side visor indicating it was produced in March or April 1942.

A new Ausf G with an application of tropical paint is in the process of being secured on a flatbed railway car. The gun barrel is darker in appearance suggesting that it still retains the dark grey heat-resistant primer.

An Ausf H advances along a road during the Kursk offensive in July 1943. This Panzer appears to be painted in olive green. By 1943, olive green was being used on vehicles, weapons and large pieces of equipment. A red-brown colour RAL 8012 was also introduced at the same time. These two colours, along with a new colour base of dark yellow RAL 7028 were issued to crews in the form a high-concentrate paste.

An Ausf H of the 3rd Panzer Division can be seen driving along a road during operations in France in 1944. Note the track lines bolted to the tank which appear to be from a US-manufactured M3 or M4 medium tank seen on both corners of the tank superstructure front plate as well as the glacis plate. Note the 'Berlin bear' divisional insignia painted in yellow on the turret *schürzen*.

The crew with their whitewashed Ausf G on board a flatbed rail car being prepared to move to the front. Transporting armour by train was the fastest way of moving units quickly from one part of the front to another, but perilously dangerous during the day.

An Ausf J with an SdKfz 251/3 Ausf C in the summer of 1944. The tactical number on the *schürzen* in red with a white outline can be seen painted next to the Balkenkreuz.

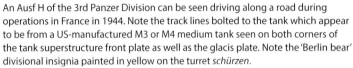

An Ausf J during operations on the Eastern Front in the summer of 1944. Note the T-34 track links bolted to the side of the hull for additional armoured protection. The Panzer has been painted in dark yellow RAL 7028 with camouflage scheme of red-brown RAL 8017 and olive green RAL 6003 spots.